Dean John Burgon's Defense of the Authorized Version

By David C. Bennett, D. Min.

Published by
THE BIBLE FOR TODAY PRESS
900 Park Avenue
Collingswood, New Jersey 08108
U.S.A.
Pastor D. A. Waite, Th.D., Ph.D.
Bible For Today Baptist Church
Church Phone: 856-854-4747
BFT Phone: 856-854-4452
Orders: 1-800-John 10:9
e-mail: BFT@BibleForToday.org
Website: www.BibleForToday.org
Fax: 856-854-2464

We Use and Defend
The King James Bible
March, 2014
BFT 4094
Copyright 2014
All Rights Reserved
ISBN #978-1-56848-105-0

Cover Design and Publishing facilitated by:
The Old Paths Publications, Inc.
www.theoldpathspublications.com
706-865-0153

Acknowledgments

I wish to acknowledge the assistance of the following people:

- **Dr. David Bennett**–the author of this book. He is one of our church's missionaries serving with his wife, Pam, in the country of Australia. This is a message that will be given at our 36th Annual Conference in July 23-24, 2014. He has strong and accurate convictions in defense of the King James Bible and the Hebrew, Aramaic, and Greek Words that underlie it.

- **Pam Bennett**–Dr. Bennett's wife who has encouraged him in his ministry in Australia and in his many articles and books the the Lord has led him to write.

- **Yvonne Sanborn Waite**--my wife, for encouraging me to publish various books, including this one. She believes, as I do, that truth must get out, especially because there is so much error regarding the make-up and importance of the Bible.

- **Anne Marie Noyle**–a faithful supporter of our **Bible For Today** ministries and an attender via the Internet of our **Bible For Today Baptist Church**, who read the book and gave many valuable suggestions.

Pastor D. A. Waite, Th.D., Ph.D.
D. A. Waite
Editor and Publisher

FOREWORD

- **The Author.** Dr. David Bennett has been one of our **Bible For Today Baptist Church's** missionaries since 1994. As mentioned in this book, he was with the Association of Baptists for World Evangelism (ABWE) as a missionary to Australia for many years, until 1994. His convictions on the King James Bible and the Hebrew, Aramaic, and Greek Words that underlie it, as well as his convictions on the teachings of Biblical separation led him to leave that mission which was heading in an unBiblical direction in both of these areas. He, and his wife, Pamela, have continued in their missionary ministry in Australia even after resigning from the ABWE missionary agency.
- **Changing His Sending Church.** In 1994, Dr. and Mrs. Bennett's convictions led them also to change their sending church to one that stood firmly both on the King James Bible, on its underlying preserved original Words, and on proper Biblical separation from both apostasy and theological compromise. We have been privileged to have the Bennetts to represent our church on the mission field of Australia from 1994 to the present.
- **The Book's Quotations From Dean John W. Burgon in His Defense of the Authorized Version.** Dr. Bennett is one of the Executive Committee members of the Dean Burgon Society (DBS). He chose to give Dean Burgon's defense of the Authorized Version at our 36th Annual Meeting in Marietta, Georgia, July 23-24, 2014. This is a valuable topic for the DBS which is named after Dean Burgon. Dr. Bennett also exposes the English Revised Version (ERV). The exhaustive Index of Words, Phrases & Scriptures will make it easy for the readers to find many details.

D. A. Waite

Pastor D. A. Waite, Th.D., Ph.D.
Director of the **Bible For Today**, Incorporated, and
Pastor of the **Bible For Today Baptist Church**

Table of Contents

Publisher's Data i

Acknowledgments ii

Foreword iii

Table of Contents iv

Introductory Considerations 1

Dean John Burgon's Defense of the Authorized Version .. 3

Appendix 1: Baptist Fellowships and the Abandonment of the King James Bible 37

Appendix 2: The English Standard Version 2011 61

    The ESV Translating Committee 65

    About the ESV Translation Philosophy 71

    Manuscripts Used in Translating the ESV ... 73

Index of Words and Phrases 85

Dean John Burgon's Defense of the Authorized Version

By David C. Bennett, D. Min.

Introductory Considerations

King James Bible Defense Needed. We're living in a day and time when a <u>proper</u> understanding of the Authorized (King James) Version (AV) is missing both by its Gnostic Critical Greek Text and new version foes and its Ruckman and Riplinger following "friends."

Dean John Burgon To The Rescue. What greater defender of our Authorized Version to call upon but Dean John William Burgon, the Dean of Chichester in England. Dean Burgon was a Bible-believing scholar who was contemporary (and of the same denomination) with the two leading non-Bible-believing apostates, Bishop Westcott and Professor Hort. The views of these two leaders have been followed by many anti-KJB opponents of our day, including many theological conservatives.

Dr. Bennett Quotes Extensively From Dean Burgon. His quotations are from Dean Burgon's master work, *The Revision Revised* which has been reprinted by the Dean Burgon Society. It is available as **BFT #595 @ $25.00 + $8.00 S&H**. Dr. Bennett also exposes one of the current most erroneous followers of the Gnostic Critical Greek Text, the English Revised Version (ERV). An extensive INDEX aids the reader in finding key words and phrases.

Dean John Burgon's Defense of the Authorized Version
By David C. Bennett, D. Min.

The Roman statesman and historian Cicero wrote: *"The first law for the historian is that he shall never dare utter an untruth. The second is that he shall suppress nothing that is true."*

This paper is based on history. Therefore it will utter nothing but the truth, and suppress nothing that is true. Personally, I am not afraid of the truth. My Saviour is Truth (John 14:6), and His Word is Truth (John 17:17)! The history of which I speak concerns first: how I came to the conviction I now hold concerning the King James Bible and its underlying Greek Text and second: what the namesake of the Dean Burgon Society (Dean Burgon himself) believed about the Textus Receptus and the King James Bible. My undergraduate degree is from Faith Baptist Bible College (FBBC)[1], Ankeny, IA. This school was not King James Only but, as with many thought to be "fundamental" independent Baptist colleges, **most** of the professors **used only** the King James Bible in the classroom. However, one professor did use the American Standard Version of 1901 in the classroom, while another professor, surprisingly a Dallas Seminary graduate, not only used the King James Bible but also authored a pamphlet defending the Received Text. Therefore, the school was sending what I now perceive to be a mixed message on the issue of what English version is the Word of God in English.

In Greek class, the King James Bible was the English Bible used, but the Greek text was the Second Edition of the United Bible Societies (UBS) Greek New Testament. This text was edited by Kurt Aland, German apostate, Matthew Black, also an apostate, Carlo M. Martini, a Roman Catholic Cardinal, Bruce M. Metzger, apostate Editor of the *Readers Digest Bible*, and Allen Wikgren, a member of the 1952 Revised Standard Version committee. These were the editors of the Greek Text used in a "fundamentalist" Baptist college! Most

---

[1] More on this in Appendix 1.

students do not realize the inconsistency here. They are using a Greek text that is the child of Westcott and Hort's Greek text and departs from the Greek text of the King James Bible in eight thousand places.[2] The students are not told, nor do they even think to ask why this inconsistency; for they are the students! With this background, I would dare say--with much sadness--that most of those graduates from my days at FBBC have probably forsaken the King James Bible for another version.

Later I enrolled in a Masters program at Grand Rapids Baptist Seminary (GRBS). I was fortunate enough that not far into the Master's program at GRBS it was detected that GRBS and I were not compatible in several areas of ministry. On that discovery I transferred along with a friend from GRBS to Bethany Theological Seminary at Dothan, Alabama. It was there I was introduced to the Church of England's Dean of Chichester, John William Burgon (August 21, 1813--August 4, 1888) and to his book, *The Revision Revised*. It was that one book **that changed my heart-held conviction regarding the Greek and English Texts of the Bible!** However, my friend was not as convinced as I was. Nevertheless, it was soon after reading this book, *The Revision Revised*, that I joined the Dean Burgon Society which exists for the sole purpose of defending the King James Bible and the Hebrew, Aramaic, and Greek Words underlying the King James Bible.

> Since joining the DBS I have read men of other opinions such as James Richard May who says:
>
> *"Burgon, Anglican Churchman and Greek scholar, was a contemporary and vigorous opponent of Westcott and Hort. While Burgon spoke highly of their character and ability, he opposed the Westcott and Hort Greek New Testament and the English Revised Version derived from it with very harsh language. KJVers make a false assumption, however, when they assume that the enemy of their enemy is their friend.*

---

[2] Dr. J. A. Moorman, *8,000 Differences*, Bible For Today & The Dean Burgon Society, 900 Park Avenue, Collingswood, NJ, 08108

> *Burgon differed with the Dean Burgon Society first in regard to the process which led to the creation of the Textus Receptus and the King James Bible, and secondly in regard to the alleged perfection of the TR and KJV. In reality, the position and teachings of John Burgon demonstrate him to be the greatest enemy of King James Onlyism."*[3]

Then there is Jeff Straub, an adjunct professor at Central Seminary, who wrote:
> *"In the late 19th century, John William Burgon and some of his associates argued for the KJV against the Revised Version—not because the KJV was a superior English translation but because the underlying Greek text was a better Greek text than the RV used (the Westcott and Hort text)."*[4]

Then there is Dallas Seminary Daniel B. Wallace who says of our DBS:
> *"The Dean Burgon Society, founded in Philadelphia on November 3-4, 1978, by D A Waite, D O Fuller and E L Bynum, also staunchly defends the TR . . . The name is a curiosity since Burgon's views would disqualify him from membership in the society named after him."*[5]

Are these three men correct? Yes and No. As I have said before in other papers, there is not a man of the seed of Adam that I totally agree with and John William Burgon would be included. Nevertheless John Burgon was a giant intellectually and as a scholar. *The Revision Revised* and the other books he and his associate, Edward Miller, wrote are the solid foundation upon which those of us who hold a high view of Scripture, the King James Bible and its underlying Hebrew, Aramaic, and Greek Words stand. **Therefore, in spite of what men such as May, Straub, Wallace and others like them say; John William Burgon's books may be read with all confidence by those who desire to know the truth and those who already hold dear the Textus Receptus and the King James Bible.**

---

[3] http://www.kjvonly.org/james/may_burgon_enemy_kjvism.htm

[4] http://baptistbulletin.org/?p=16763

[5] Daniel B. Wallace, *JOURNAL OF THE EVANGELICAL THEOLOGICAL SOCIETY*, pdf., footnote p. 2.

One of the claims made against the text underlying our King James Bible is the few manuscripts Erasmus supposedly used. The Dean's reply to this is:

> *"that the copies employed were selected because they were known to represent with accuracy the Sacred Word; that the descent of the text was evidently guarded with jealous care, just as the human genealogy of our Lord was preserved; that it rests mainly upon much the widest testimony; and that where any part of it conflicts with the fullest evidence attainable, there I believe that it calls for correction."*[6]

Oh, so Burgon did believe the text needed correction?! Well, we will let him answer for himself. In another place he said:

> *"The question therefore which presents itself, and must needs be answered in the affirmative before a single syllable of the actual text is displaced, will always be one and the same, viz. this: Is it certain that the evidence in favour of the proposed new reading is sufficient to warrant the innovation? For I trust we shall all be agreed that in the absence of an affirmative answer to this question, the text may on no account be disturbed. Rightly or wrongly it has had the approval of Western Christendom for three centuries, and is at this hour in possession of the field. Therefore the business before us might be stated somewhat as follows: What considerations ought to determine our acceptance of any reading not found in the Received Text, or, to state it more generally and fundamentally, our preference of one reading before another? For until some sort of understanding has been arrived at on this head, progress is impossible. There can be no Science of Textual Criticism, I repeat—and therefore no security for the inspired Word—so long as the subjective judgement, which may easily degenerate into individual caprice, is allowed ever to determine which readings shall be rejected, which retained."*[7]

---

[6] Dean John William Burgon, THE TRADITIONAL TEXT OF THE HOLY GOSPELS, Dean Burgon Society Press, Box 354, Collingswood, NJ, 08108, p. 15.

[7] Dean John William Burgon, THE TRADITIONAL TEXT OF THE HOLY GOSPELS, Dean Burgon Society Press, Box 354, Collingswood, NJ, 08108, pp. 5, 6.

If there were to be any changes in the text of the Word of God Dean John William Burgon had seven notes of truth by which the reading should be attested. They were;
1. *Antiquity, or Primitiveness;*
2. *Consent of Witnesses, or Number;*
3. *Variety of Evidence, or Catholicity;*
4. *Respectability of Witnesses, or Weight;*
5. *Continuity, or Unbroken Tradition;*
6. *Evidence of the Entire Passage, or Context;*
7. *Internal Considerations, or Reasonableness.*[8]

Now, as to what Dean John Burgon may have said "negatively" concerning the Textus Receptus and the need for a revision, Dr. D. A. Waite, president of the Dean Burgon Society, has sufficiently answered that allegation and his answer may read be at the address in the following footnote[9]. However, before I go further, I will allow John Burgon to briefly tell us what he truly thought of the Authorized Version. He said:

> "*We shall in fact never have another 'Authorized Version.' And this single consideration may be thought absolutely fatal to the project, except in a greatly modified form. To be brief,—As a companion in the study and for private edification: as a book of reference for critical purposes, especially in respect of difficult and controverted passages:—we hold that a revised edition of the Authorized Version of our English Bible, (if executed with consummate ability and learning,) would at any time be a work of inestimable value. The method of such a performance, whether by marginal Notes or in some other way, we forbear to determine. But certainly only as a handmaid is it to be desired. As something intended to supersede our present English Bible, we are thoroughly convinced that the project of a rival*

---

[8] *Ibid.*, p. 29.

[9] http://www.deanburgonsociety.org/DeanBurgon/dbs0804.htm

8 Dean John Burgon's Defense of the Authorized Version

> *Translation is not to be entertained for a moment. For ourselves, we deprecate it entirely.*"[10]

In this paper I will be giving quotes from John Burgon's *The Revision Rev* which will show the reader what John Burgon actually had to say concern the Authorized Version. There will be no untruth uttered nor any t suppressed! The statements are taken from a pdf of *The Revision Revised* this writer finds the pdf is much easier to copy and paste from than retyp everything from a hard copy book. However, it must be said that ther nothing quite like having a hard copy of a good book and *The Revision Rev* is such a book! *The Revision Revised* is still in print today and may be obtai from those listed in the footnote below[12].

Note also, the words **Authorized Version** will be emphasized in bold prin those statements made by John Burgon in *The Revision Revised* concerning **Authorized Version**.

Early in *The Revision Revised* on page 5 John Burgon states of Westcott Hort's (W&H) English and Greek Texts that:

"*Their uncouth phraseology and their jerky sentences, their pedantic obscurity and their unidiomatic English, contrast painfully with 'the happy turns of expression, the music of the cadences, the felicities of the rhythm' of our **Authorized Version**. The transition from one to the other, as the Bishop of Lincoln remarks, is like exchanging a well-built carriage for a vehicle without springs, in which you get jolted to death on a newly-mended and*

---

[10] John William Burgon, *The Revision Revised*, The Project Gutenberg Ebook, pdf.

[11] http://www.gutenberg.org/license

[12] http://www.deanburgonsociety.org/idx_Pages/idx_dbs_press
http://www.amazon.com/dp/1888328010

rarely-traversed road. But the 'Revised Version' is inaccurate as well; exhibits defective scholarship, I mean, in countless places."

Attention should be paid to the contrast the Bishop of Lincoln makes between the Revised Version and the Authorized Version. Again see how it is said The Revised Version is likened to a carriage without springs which jolts the rider to death! This is certainly not a recommendation for the W & H English Revision!!! What was true then in John Burgon's day is certainly true today. With the multitude of English versions on the market there is not another English translation in print today that can compare to the cadence and rhythm of the King James Bible! The children of the 1881 English Revised Version read basically just like their father!

On page 13 John Burgon states that:

> **"***on examining the so called 'Revision of the **Authorized Version**,' I speedily made the further discovery that the Revised English would have been in itself intolerable, even had the Greek been let alone."*

It is to this Revised English Version that all but the New King James Version are related. The English Standard Version (ESV) is the choice of many conservative evangelicals and, not surprisingly, it is an offshoot "... *of the RSV, with the 1971 RSV text providing the starting point. . . .*"[13] for the ESV. The outcome is like father, like son. Just like the RSV, the ESV is not based on the Received Text but is based:

> "*on the Greek text in the 1993 editions of the Greek New Testament (4th corrected ed.), published by the United Bible Societies (UBS), and Novum Testamentum Graece (27th ed.), edited by Nestle and Aland.*"[14]

Now some will argue that the Greek texts underlying the ESV and other new English translations are not in any way related to Westcott and Hort's work. However, the UBS 2nd Edition Greek New Testament states on page v that:

---

[13] http://www.esv.org/esv/translation/about/

[14] *Ibid.*

"*Westcott and Hort's edition of the Greek New Testament*" was used for comparison as was Tischendorf's and von Soden's. What company!!!!!

John Burgon stated, on page 14, that:
> "*A skittish impatience of the admirable work before them, and a strange inability to appreciate its manifold excellences:—a singular imagination on the part of the promiscuous Company which met in the Jerusalem Chamber that they were competent to improve the **Authorized Version** in every part, and an unaccountable forgetfulness that the fundamental condition under which the task of Revision had been by themselves undertaken, was that they should abstain from all but 'necessary' changes:—this proved to be only part of the offence which the Revisionists had committed.*"

On page 31 John Burgon quotes Westcott saying:
> "*One question in connexion with the **Authorized Version** I have purposely neglected. It seemed useless to discuss its REVISION. The Revision of the original Texts must precede the Revision of the Translation: and the time for this, even in the New Testament, has not yet fully come.*"

John Burgon wrote on page 32 that W & H held great expectations "*. . . that the 'New English Version' founded on this 'New Greek Text' is destined to supersede the '**Authorized Version**' of 1611.*" Fortunately, and by the overruling of the Lord, this did not happen.

Westcott and Hort's whole purpose of course was to rid the world of the "vile"[15] Textus Receptus. However, on page 33, John Burgon wrote that
> "*For it must be plain to all, that the issue which has been thus at last raised, is of the most serious character. The Authors of this new Revision of the Greek have either entitled themselves to the Church's profound reverence and abiding gratitude; or else they have laid themselves open to her gravest censure, and must experience at her hands nothing short of stern and well-merited rebuke. No middle course

---

[15] http://www.revisedstandardversion.net/text/wnp/id_3.html

> *presents itself; since assuredly to construct a new Greek Text formed no part of the Instructions which the Revisionists received at the hands of the Convocation of the Southern Province. Rather were they warned against venturing on such an experiment; the fundamental principle of the entire undertaking having been declared at the outset to be—That 'a Revision of the **Authorized Version**" is desirable; and the terms of the original Resolution of Feb. 10th, 1870, being, that the removal of 'PLAIN AND CLEAR ERRORS' was alone contemplated,—'whether in the Greek Text originally adopted by the Translators, or in the Translation made from the same.'"*

W & H were deceivers, but the followers of the new versions do not dwell on the deceitfulness of W & H in the construction of their New Greek Text! If they would be deceptive in the formation of a New Greek text why would they not have any problems in using defective manuscripts in their deception?

Again, on page 33, John Burgon reiterates

> *"Only NECESSARY changes were to be made. The first Rule of the Committee (25th May) was similar in character: viz.—'To introduce as few alterations as possible into the Text of the **Authorized Version**, consistently with faithfulness.'"*

The lovers of the new versions like to run with the fact that John Burgon did believe there were some "necessary" changes that could be made in the Greek Text underlying the King James Bible but they do not dwell on those principles laid down by him for those changes to be made. Also those changes were to be done "consistently with faithfulness"!

On page 50, in a footnote, John Burgon wrote:

> *"That to be improved, the Textus Receptus will have to be revised on entirely different 'principles' from those which are just now in fashion. Men must begin by unlearning the German prejudices of the last fifty years; and address themselves, instead, to the stern logic of facts."*

Those German prejudices are still being accepted rather than the stern logic of facts of which John Burgon spoke.

On pages 33 and 34, John Burgon wrote that:

> "The condition was enjoined upon them that whenever 'decidedly preponderating evidence' constrained their adoption of some change in 'the Text from which the **Authorized Version** was made,' they should indicate such alteration in the margin. Will it be believed that, this notwithstanding, not one of the many alterations which have been introduced into the original Text is so commemorated? On the contrary: singular to relate, the Margin is disfigured throughout with ominous hints that, had 'Some ancient authorities,' 'Many ancient authorities,' 'Many very ancient authorities,' been attended to, a vast many more changes might, could, would, or should have been introduced into the Greek Text than have been actually adopted."

To say the least John Burgon was not happy with the disfigured Margin with the many "ominous hints" of W&H's favoured "ancient authorities."

Then, on page 36, John Burgon states:

> "It can never be any question among scholars, that *a fatal error* was committed when a body of Divines, appointed to revise the *Authorized English Version* of the New Testament Scriptures, addressed themselves to the solution of an entirely different and far more intricate problem, namely the re-construction of the Greek Text."

Note the words "<u>**fatal error**</u>"! John Burgon was not a supporter of the W&H New Greek Text, but, sadly, it cannot be said of so many conservatives (including Independent Baptists) today!

Going forward to page 67 we read John Burgon as saying:

> "And thus, the men who were appointed to improve the English Translation are exhibited to us remodelling the original Greek. At a moment's notice, as if by intuition,—by an act which can only be described as the exercise of instinct,—these eminent Divines undertake to decide which shall be deemed the genuine utterances of the HOLY GHOST,—which not. Each is called upon to give his vote, and he gives it. 'The Text being thus settled'' they proceed to

> *do the only thing they were originally appointed to do; viz. to try their hands at improving our **Authorized Version**. But we venture respectfully to suggest, that by no such 'rough and ready' process is that most delicate and*
>
> > *difficult of all critical problems—the truth of Scripture—to be 'settled.''*

John Burgon saw the work of the revisers a *"most delicate and difficult one"* but definitely NOT settled by their *"rough and ready process"*!

In a footnote on page 79, John Burgon said:

> *"Dr. Scrivener has (with rare ability and immense labour) set before the Church, for the first time, the Greek Text which was followed by the Revisers of 1611, viz. Beza's N. T. of 1598, supplemented in above 190 places from other sources; every one of which the editor traces out in his Appendix, pp. 648-56. At the foot of each page, he shows what changes have been introduced into the Text by the Revisers of 1881.—Dr. Palmer, taking the Text of Stephens (1550) as his basis, presents us with the Readings adopted by the Revisers of the "**Authorized Version**," and relegates the displaced Readings (of 1611) to the foot of each page.—We cordially congratulate them both, and thank them for the good service they have rendered."*

On page 82, John Burgon tells us:

> *"Another corruption of the text, with which it is proposed henceforth to disfigure our **Authorized Version**, (originating like the last in sheer accident,) occurs in Acts xviii. 7."*

Here, in Acts 18:7, the King James Bible reads *"And he departed thence, and entered into a certain man's house, named **Justus**, one that worshipped God, whose house joined hard to the synagogue."* However, W & H's Greek and English interlinear says (kai metabas ekeithen eelthen eis oikian) "AND HAVING STEPPED ACROSS FROM THERE HE CAME INTO HOUSE (tinos onomati titiou ioustou sebomenou ton theon) OF SOMEONE TO NAME TITIUS JUSTUS VENERATING THE GOD, (hou hee oikia een sunomorousa tee sunagwgee) WHOSE THE HOUSE WAS HAVING JOINT BOUNDARY TO THE SYNAGOGUE."

14   Dean John Burgon's Defense of the Authorized Version

Of the introduction of "*Titus*" here John Burgon states, on page 83, that:
> "'*Titus Justus;*' with whose appearance,—(and he is found nowhere but in codex B,)—Tischendorf in his 8th ed., with Westcott and Hort in theirs, are so captivated, that they actually give him a place in their text. It was out of compassion (we presume) for the friendless stranger 'Titus Justus' that our Revisionists have, in preference, promoted him to honour: in which act of humanity they stand alone. Their 'new Greek Text' is the only one in existence in which the imaginary foreigner has been advanced to citizenship, and assigned 'a local habitation and a name.'"

W & H along with Tischendorf showed "*compassion*" for this "*friend stranger*"! In fact they alone have promoted this before unknown man "*T Justus*" to a place of "*honour*". Can you see the dry but serious humour which John Burgon makes his point?

Most pictures I have seen of John Burgon, he appears somewhat stern but he often shows forth his sense of humour, such as on page 83, when he says:
> "Those must have been wondrous drowsy days in the Jerusalem Chamber when such manipulations of the inspired text were possible!"

In commenting on Mark 11:8, on page 87, John Burgon writes:

> "We turn to our **Authorized Version**, and are refreshed by the familiar and intelligible words: 'And others cut down branches off the trees and strawed them in the way.' Why then has this been changed?"

Here, as the reader can see John Burgon relates the reader of Scripture "refreshed" by reading the Authorized Version as compared to the reading the Revised English Bible which says "And many spread their garments in way, and others branches which they cut out of the fields." On the same p John Burgon humourously remarked "They must have been clever pe certainly if they 'cut branches from' anything except trees."

On page 105, the Dean writes:
> "*all should have been passed by in silence, but that unhappily the 'Revision' of our **Authorized Version** is touched thereby very nearly indeed. So intimate (may we not say, so fatal?) proves to be the sympathy between the labours of Drs. Westcott and Hort and those of our Revisionists, that whatever the former have shut up within double brackets, the latter are discovered to have branded with a note of suspicion, conceived invariably in the same terms: viz., 'Some ancient authorities omit.' And further, whatever those Editors have rejected from their Text, these Revisionists have rejected also.*"

The revision of 1881 brought in a flood of suspicion on the text of Scripture so that now many schools whose primary purpose is to teach the Bible are not sure if they have the Bible!

On pages 116 and 117, John Burgon tells us:
> "*the Revisionists who assure us 'that they did not esteem it within their province to construct a continuous and complete Greek Text;' (and who were never authorized to construct a new Greek Text at all;) were not justified in the course they have pursued with regard to S. Luke xxiii. 38. 'THIS IS THE KING OF THE JEWS' is the only idiomatic way of rendering into English the title according to S. Luke, whether the reading of A or of B be adopted; but, in order to make it plain that they reject the Greek of A in favour of B, the Revisionists have gone out of their way. They have instructed the two Editors of 'The Greek Testament with the Readings adopted by the Revisers of the **Authorized Version**' to exhibit S. Luke xxiii. 38 as it stands in the mutilated recension of Drs. Westcott and Hort. And if this procedure, repeated many hundreds of times, be not constructing a 'new Greek Text' of the N. T., we have yet to learn what is.*"

As most readers of this paper know the words W & H deleted from verse 38 were "*was written,*" "*in letters of Greek, and Latin, and Hebrew*" and the word "*is.*" As John Burgon stated above "*the only idiomatic way of rendering into English the title according to S. Luke*" was the way of the Textus Receptus but W & H in their Greek Text placed "*This*" at the end of "*the king of the jews*" reading thus "*the king of the jews THIS.*" Of course W & H added the note in the English Revised Version that the "*Rec. Text adds in letters of Greek and Latin and Hebrew.*" All of this to throw suspicion on the Words of God.

On page 118, commenting on Luke 24:10 and the words "*It was Mary Magdalene, and Joanna, and Mary the mother of James, and other women with them, which told these things unto the Apostles*" John Burgon said the lack of "*and certain others with them*" in Luke 24:1 was originally the result of:
> "some stupid harmonizer in the IInd century omitted the words, because they were in his way. Calamitous however it is that a clause which the Church has long since deliberately reinstated should, in the year 1881, be as deliberately banished for the second time from the sacred page by our Revisionists; who under the plea of amending our English **Authorized Version** have (with the best intentions) falsified the Greek Text of the Gospels in countless places,—often, as here, without notice and without apology."

The Revisionists, following what John Burgon calls the "*stupid harmonizer*" of the 2nd century, translated their 1881 Revised Version thus: "*24. But on the first day of the week, very early in the morning, they came unto the sepulchre, bringing the spices which they had prepared*.*" Of course the Revisionists give a note saying "*Rec. text adds and certain others with them.*" Whether the note was meant to intentionally throw doubt on the Received Text or not, it did and still does.

The ever so popular ESV of the new fundamentalists reads much the same as the 1881 Revised saying: "*24 But on the first day of the week, at early dawn, they went to the tomb, taking the spices they had prepared.*" The NIV follows suit reading: "*24 On the first day of the week, very early in the morning, the women took the spices they had prepared and went to the tomb.*" These new versions only change enough from the other versions based on the Critical Text so as to be copyrighted and profit from the change.

On pages 135 and 136, John Burgon wrote:
> ". . . we have thoroughly convinced ourselves that the 'new Greek Text' put forth by the Revisionists of our Authorized Version is utterly inadmissible. The traditional Text has been

departed from by them nearly 6000 times,—almost invariably for the worse."
NEARLY 6,000 TIMES AND NOT FOR THE BETTER BUT FOR THE WORSE!

On pages 138 and 139, we read John Burgon saying:
*"In a future number, we may perhaps enquire into the measure of success which has attended the Revisers' Revision of the English of our **Authorized Version** of 1611. We have occupied ourselves at this time exclusively with a survey of the seriously mutilated and otherwise grossly depraved NEW GREEK TEXT, on which their edifice has been reared. And the circumstance which, in conclusion, we desire to impress upon our Readers, is this,—that the insecurity of that foundation is so alarming, that, except as a concession due to the solemnity of the undertaking just now under review, further Criticism might very well be dispensed with, as a thing superfluous. Even could it be proved concerning the superstructure, that 'it had been [ever so] well builded,' (to adopt another of our Revisionists' unhappy perversions of Scripture,) the fatal objection would remain, viz. that it is not 'founded upon the rock.'"*
WHAT THEN CAN BE SAID OF ALL THOSE ENGLISH VERSIONS PRODUCED FROM THOSE GREEK TEXTS SPAWNED FROM W & H'S NEW GREEK TEXT!?

On page 140, John Burgon quotes Bishop Ellicott: *"No Revision at the present day could hope to meet with an hour's acceptance if it failed to preserve the tone, rhythm, and diction of the present Authorized Version."*

The next page over, page 141, John Burgon states that:
*"Whatever may be urged in favour of Biblical Revision, it is at least undeniable that the undertaking involves a tremendous risk. Our **Authorized Version** is the one religious link which at present binds together ninety millions of English-speaking men scattered over the earth's surface. Is it reasonable that so unutterably precious, so sacred a bond should be endangered, for the sake of representing certain words more accurately,—here and there translating a tense*

18   Dean John Burgon's Defense of the Authorized Version

> *with greater precision,—getting rid of a few archaisms? It may be confidently assumed that no "Revision" of our **Authorized Version**, however judiciously executed, will ever occupy the place in public esteem which is actually enjoyed by the work of the Translators of 1611,—the noblest literary work in the Anglo-Saxon language. We shall in fact never have another "**Authorized Version.**" And this single consideration may be thought absolutely fatal to the project, except in a greatly modified form. To be brief,—As a companion in the study and for private edification: as a book of reference for critical purposes, especially in respect of difficult and controverted passages:—we hold that a revised edition of the **Authorized Version** of our English Bible, (if executed with consummate ability and learning,) would at any time be a work of inestimable value. The method of such a performance, whether by marginal Notes or in some other way, we forbear to determine. But certainly only as a handmaid is it to be desired. As something intended to supersede our present English Bible, we are thoroughly convinced that the project of a rival Translation is not to be entertained for a moment. For ourselves, we deprecate it entirely."*

Did you read that last statement! John Burgon said "<u>we are thoroughly convinced that the project of a rival Translation is not to be entertained for a moment. For ourselves, we deprecate it entirely</u>." To "*deprecate*" is to "*disapprove*"!

On pages 141 and 142 John Burgon wrote:
> "*who could have possibly foreseen what has actually come to pass since the Convocation of the Southern Province (in Feb. 1870) declared itself favourable to 'a Revision of the **Authorized Version**,' and appointed a Committee of Divines to undertake the work? Who was to suppose that the Instructions given to the Revisionists would be by them systematically disregarded? Who was to imagine that an utterly untrustworthy 'new Greek Text,' constructed on mistaken principles,—(say rather, on no principles at all,)—would be the fatal result?*"

Does it need to be asked what John Burgon thought of the W & H New Greek Text?!

Next, is a lengthy quotation, but it is worth the read. On pages 152 & 153, John Burgon tells us what MUST be done before any revision is even begun on the Greek Text in use before the W & H Critical Text. He wrote:

*"The fundamental Principles of the Science of Textual Criticism are not yet apprehended. In proof of this assertion, we appeal to the new Greek Text of Drs. Westcott and Hort,—which, beyond all controversy, is more hopelessly remote from the inspired Original than any which has yet appeared. Let a generation of Students give themselves entirely up to this neglected branch of sacred Science. Let 500 more COPIES of the Gospels, Acts, and Epistles, be diligently collated. Let at least 100 of the ancient Lectionaries be very exactly collated also. Let the most important of the ancient VERSIONS be edited afresh, and let the languages in which these are written be for the first time really mastered by Englishmen. Above all, let the FATHERS he called upon to give up their precious secrets. Let their writings be ransacked and indexed, and (where needful) let the MSS. of their works be diligently inspected, in order that we may know what actually is the evidence which they afford. Only so will it ever be possible to obtain a Greek Text on which absolute reliance may be placed, and which may serve as the basis for a satisfactory Revision of our **Authorized Version**. Nay, let whatever unpublished works of the ancient Greek Fathers are anywhere known to exist,—(and not a few precious remains of theirs are lying hid in great national libraries, both at home and abroad,)—let these be printed. The men could easily be found: the money, far more easily.—When all this has been done,—not before—then in GOD'S Name, let the Church address herself to the great undertaking. Do but revive the arrangements which were adopted in King James's days: and we venture to predict that less than a third part of ten years will be found abundantly to suffice for the work."*

On page 154, we read:
> "TO INTRODUCE AS FEW ALTERATIONS AS POSSIBLE INTO THE TEXT OF THE **AUTHORIZED VERSION**, CONSISTENTLY WITH FAITHFULNESS.' Words could not be more emphatic. 'PLAIN AND CLEAR ERRORS' were to be corrected. 'NECESSARY emendations' were to be made. But (in the words of the Southern Convocation) 'We do not contemplate any new Translation, or any alteration of the language, EXCEPT WHERE, in the judgment of the most competent Scholars, SUCH CHANGE IS NECESSARY.' The watchword, therefore, given to the company of Revisionists was,—'NECESSITY.' Necessity was to determine whether they were to depart from the language of the **Authorized Version**, or not; for the alterations were to be AS FEW AS POSSIBLE."

John Burgon wrote on page 162:
> "Shame,—yes, shame on the learning which comes abroad only to perplex the weak, and to unsettle the doubting, and to mislead the blind! Shame,—yes, shame on that two-thirds majority of well-intentioned but most incompetent men, who,—finding themselves (in an evil hour) appointed to correct 'plain and clear errors' in the English '**Authorized Version**,'—occupied themselves instead with falsifying the inspired Greek Text in countless places, and branding with suspicion some of the most precious utterances of the SPIRIT! Shame,—yes, shame upon them!"

John Burgon was kind in calling the Revisers "*well-intentioned*" but he then turns the tables and calls them the "*most incompetent men.*" Whether the first was true or not the second certainly was.

On page 166, John Burgon quotes the Revisers:
> "If the meaning was fairly expressed by the word or phrase that was before us in the Authorized Version, we made no change, even where rigid adherence to the rule of Translating, as far as possible, the same Greek word by the same English word might have prescribed some modification."

Dean John Burgon's Defense of the Authorized Version

John Burgon was quite perturbed that the Revisers seemed to be intent on making changes to just make changes. He wrote on page 177:

> "*The perfectly accurate rendering of S. Matthew. xxvi. 15, therefore, exhibited by our **Authorized Version**, has been set aside to make way for a misrepresentation of the Evangelist's meaning. 'In the judgment of the most competent scholars,' was 'such change NECESSARY'?*
>
> *(g) We respectfully think that it would have been more becoming in such a company as that which assembled in the Jerusalem Chamber, as well as more consistent with their Instructions, if in doubtful cases they had abstained from touching the **Authorized Version**, but had recorded their own conjectural emendations in the margin.*"

John Burgon tells the reader on page 181 that:

> "*what supremely annoys us in the work just now under review is, that the schoolboy method of translation already noticed is therein exhibited in constant operation throughout. It becomes oppressive. We are never permitted to believe that we are in the company of Scholars who are altogether masters of their own language. Their solicitude ever seems to be twofold:—(1) To exhibit a singular indifference to the proprieties of English speech, while they maintain a servile adherence (etymological or idiomatic, as the case may be) to the Greek:—(2) Right or wrong, to part company from William Tyndale and the giants who gave us our 'Authorized Version.'*"

Truly, there were GIANTS in the land preceding and including the translation of the Authorized Version!

We now turn to page 184. John Burgon writes concerning the Revisers change in John 17:4 & 6:

> "*We turn to the place indicated, and are constrained to assure these well-intentioned men, that the phenomenon we there witness is absolutely fatal to their pretensions as 'Revisers' of our **Authorized Version**. Were it only 'some passing difficulty' which their method occasions us, we might have hoped that time would enable us to overcome it. But since it is the genius of the English language to which we*

find they have offered violence; the fixed and universally-understood idiom of our native tongue which they have systematically set at defiance; the matter is absolutely without remedy. The difference between the A. V. and the R. V. seems to ourselves to be simply this,—that the renderings in the former are the idiomatic English representations of certain well-understood Greek tenses: while the proposed substitutes are nothing else but the pedantic efforts of mere grammarians to reproduce in another language idioms which it abhors. But the Reader shall judge for himself: for this at least is a point on which every educated Englishman is fully competent to pass sentence."

AV John 17:4 *"I have glorified thee on the earth: I **have finished** the work which thou gavest me to do."* John 17:6 *"I have manifested thy name unto the men **which thou gavest** me out of the world: thine they were, and **thou gavest** them me; and they have kept thy word."*

RV John 17:4. *"I have glorified thee on the earth, **having finished** the work which thou gavest me to do."* 17:6. *"I have manifested thy name unto the men '**whom thou hast given** me out of the world; thine they were, and **thou hast given** them unto me ; and they have kept thy word."*

NIV John 17:4. *"I have brought you glory on earth by **finishing** the work you gave me to do."* 17:6 *"I have revealed you to those **whom you gave** me out of the world. They were yours; **you gave** them to me and they have obeyed your word."*

ESV John 17:4. *"I glorified you on earth, **having accomplished** the work that you gave me to do."* 17:6 *"I have manifested your name to the people **whom you gave** me out of the world. Yours they were, and **you gave** them to me, and they have kept your word."*[16]

Further down on page 184, John Burgon states his disgust for the Reviser's changes in John 17: 4 & 6 by saying

"*there can be no doubt whatever that, had He pronounced those words in English, He would have said (with our A. V.)*

---

[16] Appendix 2

> *"I have glorified Thee on the earth: I have finished the work:" "I have manifested Thy Name." The pedantry which (on the plea that the Evangelist employs the aorist, not the perfect tense,) would twist all this into the indefinite past,—"I glorified" ... "I finished" ... "I manifested,"—we pronounce altogether insufferable. We absolutely refuse it a hearing."*

It can be assured he would have the same disgust for the neo-fundamentalist's ESV's rendering.

Going to page 187, concerning Luke 5:4, John Burgon states that:
> *"On the other hand, there are occasions confessedly when the Greek Aorist absolutely demands to be rendered into English by the sign of the Pluperfect."*

One instance of this John Burgon says is *"where our Revisionists are found to retain the idiomatic rendering of our **Authorized Version**,—'When He had left speaking.'"*

I will let my friends in the DBS who are Greek scholars deal with this, but later on the same page John Burgon writes:
> *"The R. V. has shown less consideration in S. Jo. xviii. 24,—where 'Now Annas had sent Him bound unto Caiaphas the high priest,' is right, and wanted no revision."* The RV reads in John 18:24 "Annas therefore sent him bound unto Caiaphas the high priest."

On page 198, John Burgon relates that:
> *"The foregoing strikes us as a singular illustration of the Revisionists' statement (Preface, iii. 2),—'We made no change if the meaning was fairly expressed by the word or phrase that was before us in the Authorized Version.' To ourselves it appears that every one of those 30 changes is a change for the worse; and that one of the most exquisite passages in the N. T. has been hopelessly spoiled,—rendered in fact well-nigh unintelligible,—by the pedantic officiousness of the Revisers."*

The "foregoing" passage John Burgon was referring to was 2 Peter 1:5-7 which reads in the Authorized Version as:

> "5 And beside this, giving all diligence, add to your faith virtue; and to virtue knowledge; 6 And to knowledge temperance; and to temperance patience; and to patience godliness; 7 And to godliness brotherly kindness; and to brotherly kindness charity."

The RV reads:
> "5 Yea, and for this very cause adding on your part all diligence, in **your** faith supply virtue ; and in **your** virtue knowledge ; 6 and in **your** knowledge temperance; and in **your** temperance patience ; and in **your** patience godliness ; 7 and in **your** godliness love of the brethren ; and in **your** love of the brethren love."

From this, one readily understands John Burgon's belief that they were "*a change for the worse.*"

On page 198, John Burgon tells the reader that:
> "*We must needs advert again to the ominous admission made in the Revisionists' Preface (iii. 2 init.), that to some extent they recognized the duty of a 'rigid adherence to the rule of translating, as far as possible, the same Greek word by the same English word.' This mistaken principle of theirs lies at the root of so much of the mischief which has befallen the **Authorized Version**, that it calls for fuller consideration at our hands than it has hitherto (viz. at pp. 138 and 152) received.*"

John Burgon then takes several pages giving the reader some of his "consideration" on the subject and then on the same subject matter he states, on page 216:
> "*But if the learned men who gave us our **A. V.** may be thought to have erred on the side of excess, there can be no doubt whatever, (at least among competent judges,) that our Revisionists have sinned far more grievously and with greater injury to the Deposit, by their slavish proclivity to the opposite form of error. We must needs speak out plainly: for the question before us is not, What defects are discoverable in our **Authorized Version?**—but, What amount of gain would be likely to accrue to the Church if the present*

Dean John Burgon's Defense of the Authorized Version 25

> Revision were accepted as a substitute? And we assert without hesitation, that the amount of certain loss would so largely outweigh the amount of possible gain, that the proposal may not be seriously entertained for a moment."

Later in the same paragraph John Burgon says the Revised Version was "*an utter failure.*"

Going to page 218, we read

> "These are many words, but we know not how to make them fewer. Let this one example, (only because it is the first which presented itself,) stand for a thousand others. Apart from the grievous lack of Taste (not to say of Scholarship) which such a method betrays,—who sees not that the only excuse which could have been invented for it has disappeared by the time we reach the end of our investigation? If αitεw, αitoumαi had been invariably translated 'ask,' 'ask for,' it might at least have been pretended that 'the English Reader is in this way put entirely on a level with the Greek Scholar;'—though it would have been a vain pretence, as all must admit who understand the power of language. Once make it apparent that just in a single place, perhaps in two, the Translator found himself forced to break through his rigid uniformity of rendering,—and what remains but an uneasy suspicion that then there must have been a strain put on the Evangelists' meaning in a vast proportion of the other seventy places where αitein occurs? An unlearned reader confidence in his guide vanishes; and he finds that he has had not a few deflections from the **Authorized Version** thrust upon him, of which he reasonably questions alike the taste and the necessity,—e.g. at S. Matthew xx. 20."

John Burgon furthers this matter on pages 218 and 219, writing:

> "But take a more interesting example. In S. Mark I. 18, the A. V. has, 'and straightway they forsook' (which the Revisionists alter into 'left') 'their nets.' Why? Because in verse 20, the same word αfεvτεz will recur; and because the Revisionists propose to let the statement ('they left their father Zebedee') stand. They 'level up' accordingly; and

plume themselves on their consistency. We venture to point out, however, that the verb afienai is one of a large family of verbs which,—always retaining their own essential signification,—yet depend for their English rendering entirely on the context in which they occur."

Still on page 219, John Burgon said:
"*the Revisionists of 1881 agreed the word afienai has eight diversities of meaning rightly rendered 'to suffer,' in S. Matthew iii. 15;—'to leave,' in iv. 11;—'to let have,' in v. 40;—'to forgive,' in vi. 12, 14, 15;—'to let,' in vii. 4;—'to yield up,' in xxvii. 50;—'to let go, in S. Mark xi. 6;—'to let alone,' in xiv. 6 in our Authorized Version but in order to render afienai as often as possible 'leave,' they do violence to many a place of Scripture where some other word would have been more appropriate.*"

On pages 234 & 235, John Burgon rebukes the Revisionists for their footnote on Roman 9: 5 which said:
"*Some modern Interpreters place a full stop after flesh, and translate, He who is God over all be (is) blessed for ever: or, He who is over all is God, blessed for ever. Others punctuate, flesh, who is over all. God be (is) blessed for ever.*"
" *Now this is a matter,—let it be clearly observed,—which, (as Dr. Hort is aware,) 'belongs to Interpretation,—and not to Textual Criticism.' What business then has it in these pages at all? Is it then the function of Divines appointed to revise the **Authorized Version**, to give information to the 90 millions of English-speaking Christians scattered throughout the world as to the unfaithfulness of 'some modern Interpreters'?*"

Our Authorized Bible reads in Romans 9:5: "*Whose are the fathers, and of whom as concerning the flesh Christ came, who is over all, God blessed for ever. Amen.*"

Dean John Burgon's Defense of the Authorized Version 27

Romans 9: 5 in the Revised Standard Version reads "*to them belong the patriarchs, and of their race, according to the flesh, is the Christ. God who is over all be blessed for ever. Amen.*" Note the full-stop after Christ!

Romans 9:5 in the NIV reads "*Theirs are the patriarchs, and from them is traced the human ancestry of the Messiah, who is God over all, forever praised![a] Amen.*" The NIV then has the following footnote "*Messiah, who is over all. God be forever praised! Or Messiah. God who is over all be forever praised!*"

John Burgon continues his dislike for the Revisionist's note here in Romans 9:5. On page 238, he states:

"*We shall have every Christian reader with us in our contention, that such perverse imaginations of 'modern Interpreters' are not entitled to a place in the margin of the N. T.*"

On page 247, John Burgon reiterates that the Revisionists were:

"*Charged 'to introduce as few alterations as possible into the Text of the Authorized Version,' they have on the contrary evidently acted throughout on the principle of making as many changes in it as they conveniently could.*"

John Burgon states, on pages 247 and 248, that the Revisionists were:

"*Directed 'to limit, as far as possible, the expression of to the language of the **Authorized** and earlier English Versions,'—they have introduced such terms as 'assassin,' 'apparition,' 'boon,' 'disparagement,' 'divinity,' 'effulgence,' 'epileptic,' 'fickleness,' 'gratulation,' 'irksome,' 'interpose,' 'pitiable,' 'sluggish,' 'stupor,' 'surpass,' 'tranquil:' such compounds as 'self-control,' 'world-ruler:' such phrases as 'draw up a narrative:' 'the impulse of the steersman:' 'in lack of daily food:' 'exercising oversight.' These are but a very few samples of the offence committed by our Revisionists, of which we complain.*"

Note the word "*offence*" for John Burgon was in no way pleased with the alterations made by the 1881 Revisionists!

On page 250, we read John Burgon's plea that:
> "*Linked with all our holiest, happiest memories, and bound up with all our purest aspirations: part and parcel of whatever there is of good about us: fraught with men's hopes of a blessed Eternity and many a bright vision of the never-ending Life;—the **Authorized Version**, wherever it was possible, should have been jealously retained.*"

John Burgon writes, on page 251, that:
> "*in fact the distinguished Chairman of the New Testament Company (Bishop Ellicott,) has delivered himself on this subject in language which leaves nothing to be desired, and which we willingly make our own. 'No Revision' (he says) 'in the present day could hope to meet with an hour's acceptance if it failed to preserve the tone, rhythm, and diction of the present Authorized Version.*'"

On pages 251 and 252, John Burgon pleas that:
> "*Partisanship, (which at present prevails to an extraordinary extent, but which is wondrously out of place in this department of Sacred Learning,)—Partisanship must be completely outlived,—before the Church can venture, with the remotest prospect of a successful issue, to organize another attempt at revising the **Authorized Version** of the New Testament Scriptures.*"

As if we in the DBS did not already believe it, John Burgon encourages us, on page 256:
> "*Not the least service which the Revisionists have rendered has been the proof their work affords, how very seldom our **Authorized Version** is materially wrong: how faithful and trustworthy, on the contrary, it is throughout.*"

We in the DBS would have left out the words "*very seldom,*" but this is still a triumph for the King James Bible, especially when one reads and compares the descendants of W & H's English Revised Standard Version with our faithful and trustworthy King James Bible!

Dean John Burgon's Defense of the Authorized Version 29

On pages 258 and 259, John Burgon lamented
> "*Proposing to ourselves (May 17th, 1881) to enquire into the merits of the recent Revision of the **Authorized Version** of the New Testament Scriptures, we speedily became aware that an entirely different problem awaited us and demanded preliminary investigation. We made the distressing discovery, that the underlying Greek Text had been completely refashioned throughout.*"

That was the real intent of W & H; to dethrone the Greek Text underlying the Authorized Version!

In a footnote, on page 269, John Burgon defends Dr. Scrivener by saying:
> "*No one who attends ever so little to the subject can require to be assured that 'The New Testament in the Original Greek, according to the text followed in the Authorized Version, together with the variations adopted in the Revised Version,' edited by Dr. Scrivener for the Syndics of the Cambridge University Press, 1881, does not by any means represent his own views. The learned Prebendary merely edited the decisions of the two-thirds majority of the Revisionists,—which were not his own.*"

John Burgon, writing prophetically, on page 365:
> "*Who will venture to predict the amount of mischief which must follow, if the 'New Greek Text' which has been put forth by the men who were appointed to revise the English **Authorized Version**, should become used in our Schools and in our Colleges. . . .*"

We have seen the mischief this New Greek Text and its grandchildren have caused in all denominations but especially our Baptist churches.

On page 386, John Burgon quotes Bishop Ellicott's pamphlet *In Defense Of The Revisers and Their Greek Text of the New Testament*:
> "*Nothing is more satisfactory at the present time than the evident feelings of veneration for our **Authorized Version**, and the very generally-felt desire for as little change as possible.*"

Further down on page 386, John Burgon quotes Bishop Wordsworth:
> "*Whether the Church of England,—which in her Synod, so far as this Province is concerned, sanctioned a Revision of her **Authorized Version** under the express condition, which she most wisely imposed, that no Changes should be made in it except what were absolutely necessary,—could consistently accept a Version in which 36,000 changes have been made; not a fiftieth of which can be shown to be needed, or even desirable.*"

Again quoting Ellicott, on page 418:
> "*Let us turn to the Rule. It is simply as follows:—'That the text to be adopted be that for which the Evidence is decidedly preponderating: and that when the text so adopted differs from that from which the **Authorized Version** was made, the alteration be indicated in the margin.'*"

The following is a LONG quote, from pages 418 and 419, where John Burgon wrote to Ellicott:
> "*But you seem to have forgotten that the 'Rule' which you quote formed no part of the 'Instructions' which were imposed upon you by Convocation. It was one of the 'Principles agreed to by the Committee' (25 May, 1870),—a Rule of your own making therefore,—for which Convocation neither was nor is responsible. The 'fundamental Resolutions adopted by the Convocation of Canterbury' (3rd and 5th May, 1870), five in number, contain no authorization whatever for making changes in the Greek Text. They have reference only to the work of revising 'the **Authorized Version**:' an undertaking which the first Resolution declares to be 'desirable.' 'In order to ascertain what were the Revisers' Instructions with regard to the Greek Text,' we must refer to the original Resolution of Feb. 10th, 1870: in which the removal of 'plain and clear errors, whether in the Greek Text originally adopted by the Translators, or in the Translation made from the same,'—is for the first and last time mentioned. That you yourself accepted this as the limit of your authority, is proved by your Speech in Convocation. 'We may be satisfied' (you said) 'with the attempt to correct

plain and clear errors: but there, it is our duty to stop.'
Now I venture to assert that not one in a hundred of the alterations you have actually made, 'whether in the Greek Text originally adopted by the Translators, or in the Translation made from the same,' are corrections of 'plain and clear errors.' Rather,—(to adopt the words of the learned Bishop of Lincoln,)—'I fear we must say in candour that in the Revised Version we meet in every page with **changes** which seem almost to be made *for the sake of change.*'"
ONLY FOR THE SAKE OF CHANGE! SURELY NOT!

On pages 516 and 517, John Burgon wrote:
"*I candidly avow that it was in my account a serious breach of Church order that, on engaging in so solemn an undertaking as the Revision of the **Authorized Version**, a body of Divines professing to act under the authority of the Southern Convocation should spontaneously associate with themselves Ministers of various denominations,—Baptists, Congregationalists, Wesleyan Methodists, Independents, and the like: and especially that a successor of the Apostles should have presided over the deliberations of this assemblage of Separatists. In my humble judgment, we shall in vain teach the sinfulness of Schism, if we show ourselves practically indifferent on the subject, and even set an example of irregularity to our flocks.*"
As a Baptist this is hard to swallow but that is what he wrote.

John Burgon wrote the above to say:
"*All this, however, is as nothing in comparison of the scandal occasioned by the co-option into your body of Dr. G. Vance Smith, the Unitarian Minister of S. Saviour's Gate Chapel, York.*"

On pages 518 and 519, John Burgon reiterates his disapproval of a Unitarian serving on the Revision Committee by writing:
"*Now therefore that you re-open the question, I will not scruple publicly to repeat that it seems to me nothing else but an insult to our Divine Master and a wrong to the Church,*

> that the most precious part of our common Christian heritage, the pure Word of GOD, should day by day, week by week, month by month, year after year, have been thus handled; for the avowed purpose of producing a Translation which should supersede our **Authorized Version**. That the individual in question contributed aught to your deliberations has never been pretended. On the contrary. No secret has been made of the fact that he was, (as might have been anticipated from his published writings,) the most unprofitable member of the Revising body. Why then was he at first surreptitiously elected? and why was his election afterwards stiffly maintained? The one purpose achieved by his continued presence among you was that it might be thereby made to appear that the Church of England no longer insists on Belief in the eternal Godhead of our LORD, as essential; but is prepared to surrender her claim to definite and unequivocal dogmatic teaching in respect of Faith in the Blessed TRINITY."

Does this say something about W & H?

A footnote, at the bottom of page 518, reads
> "An Unitarian Reviser of our Authorized Version, intolerable: an earnest Remonstrance and Petition,—addressed to yourself by your present correspondent:—Oxford, Parker, 1872, pp. 8."

Perhaps this is one of the reasons the New Greek Text, the Revised Standard Version and their descendants seem to weaken the deity of our Saviour.

In a footnote on pages 519, 520 we read:
> "... when a Resolution was moved and carried by the Bp. (Wilberforce) of Winchester,— 'That it is the judgment of this House that no person who denies the Godhead of our LORD JESUS CHRIST {FNS ought to be invited to join either company to which is committed the Revision of the **Authorized Version** of Holy Scripture: and that it is further the judgment of this House that any such person now on either Company should cease to act therewith. 'And that this Resolution be communicated to the Lower House, and their concurrence requested:'"—which was done.'"

Dean John Burgon's Defense of the Authorized Version

Before we leave the personage of the Unitarian Smith, but moving ahead to page 526, where we read that:

"... *the Bishops of Lincoln of 1611 were Revisers: the Vance Smiths stood without and found fault. But in the affair of 1881, Dr. Vance Smith revises, and ventilates heresy from within.* . . . "

Again, a long quote from John Burgon, where he wrote on pages 520 and 521, that he was:

"*Not unaware...that it has nevertheless been once and again confidently predicted in public Addresses, Lectures, Pamphlets, that ultimate success is in store for the Revision of 1881. I cannot but regard it as a suspicious circumstance that these vaticinations have hitherto invariably proceeded from members of the Revising body. It would ill become such an one as myself to pretend to skill in forecasting the future. But of this at least I feel certain:—that if, in an evil hour, (quod absit!), the Church of England shall ever be induced to commit herself to the adoption of the present Revision, she will by so doing expose herself to the ridicule of the rest of Christendom, as well as incur irreparable harm and loss. And such a proceeding on her part will be inexcusable, for she has been at least faithfully forewarned. Moreover, in the end, she will most certainly have to retrace her steps with sorrow and confusion. Those persons evidently overlook the facts of the problem, who refer to what happened in the case of the* **Authorized Version** *when it originally appeared, some 270 years ago; and argue that as the Revision of 1611 at first encountered opposition, which yet it ultimately overcame, so must it fare in the end with the present Revised Version also. Those who so reason forget that the cases are essentially dissimilar.*

If the difference between the **Authorized Version** *of 1611 and the Revision of 1881 were only this.—That the latter is characterized by a mechanical, unidiomatic, and even repulsive method of rendering; which was not only unattempted, but repudiated by the Authors of the earlier work;—there would have been something to urge on behalf of the later performance.*

> The plea of zeal for GOD'S Word,—a determination at all hazards to represent with even servile precision the ipsissima verba of Evangelists and Apostles,—this plea might have been plausibly put forward: and, to some extent, it must have been allowed,—although a grave diversity of opinion might reasonably have been entertained as to what constitutes 'accuracy' and 'fidelity' of translation."

In a footnote on page 524, we read:
> "The Revisers, (I say it for the last time,) were clearly going beyond their prescribed duty when they set about handling the **Authorized Version** after this merciless fashion. Their business was to correct 'plain and clear errors,'—not to produce a 'New English Version.'"

On page 525, John Burgon clearly saw that:
> "The cheapest copies of our **Authorized Version** at least exhibit the Word of GOD faithfully and helpfully. Could the same be said of a cheap edition of the work of the Revisionists,—destitute of headings to the Chapters, and containing no record of the extent to which the Sacred Text has undergone depravation throughout?"

On page 526, we read the Dean saying:
> "Disappointed men are said to have been conspicuous among the few assailants of our '**Authorized Version**,'—Scholars (as Hugh Broughton) who considered themselves unjustly overlooked and excluded. But on the present occasion, among the multitude of hostile voices, there is not a single instance known of a man excluded from the deliberations of the Jerusalem Chamber, who desired to share them. To argue therefore concerning the prospects of the Revision of 1881 from the known history of our **Authorized Version** of 1611, is to argue concerning things essentially dissimilar. With every advance made in the knowledge of the subject, it may be confidently predicted that there will spring up increased **distrust** of the Revision of 1881, and **an ever increasing aversion** from it."

The Revision of 1881 never did gain any popularity to speak of among the people as there certainly was a great "*distrust*" and with that "*an ever increasing aversion*" to it! John Burgon had written earlier on page 12 of The Revision Revised that he;

> "*knew that the 'New Greek Text,' (and therefore the 'New English Version'), had received its death-blow. It might for a few years drag out a maimed existence; eagerly defended by some,—timidly pleaded for by others. But such efforts could be of no avail. Its days were already numbered. The effect of more and yet more learned investigation,—of more elaborate and more extended inquiry,—must be to convince mankind more and yet more thoroughly that the principles on which it had been constructed were radically unsound. In the end, when partisanship had cooled down, and passion had evaporated, and prejudice had ceased to find an auditory, the 'Revision' of 1881 must come to be universally regarded as—what it most certainly is,—the most astonishing, as well as the most calamitous literary blunder of the Age.*"

My personal opinion is that this "*aversion*" to any Bible other than the Authorized Version continued especially among the "fundamental" Baptists in America until the appearance of the NIV and, in the 21st century, the ESV. Yes, the ASV was accepted earlier by some Baptists but never to the extent that many "fundamental" Baptists have today accepted the ESV.

Now, one of the major reasons why this move has eventually taken place among the "fundamental" Baptists is owed to the almost exclusive use of the Critical Greek Text being employed in these "fundamental" Baptist schools. Think about it: if the future preachers are taught that the Critical Text is the better text they will take that belief with them into the churches. Eventually there will be a change in the pew. The Christian in the pew will follow the preacher and exchange their Authorized Version to one of the new versions based on the Critical text.

It was interesting to read what Westcott wrote sixteen years after the publishing of the New Revised English Bible that:

> "*The revisers have no reason to complain of the reception which their labours have found. It does not appear that the*

> *'Authorised' Version made more rapid progress in public favour in the sixteen years after its publication ; and, as far as I can judge, the Revised Version is more commonly used by preachers now than the 'Authorised' Version was after the same period of trial* (Emphasis added)."[17]

Well, Westcott was both right and wrong. The English Revised Version was never truly accepted by the English speaking people but the Critical Greek Text was accepted by the English and the American "scholars" almost without question. The Critical Greek Text has been accepted as the best Greek Text by liberals, conservatives, new evangelicals, and many fundamentalists. From the W & H Critical Greek Text has been spawned several revised Critical Greek texts from which have come a multitude of English Versions. Many of these versions have in time found a home within many "fundamental" and conservative Baptist schools and churches.

Nevertheless, in spite of the inroads the W & H's Critical Greek text has made the Lord continues to use Dean John William Burgon, *The Revision Revised*, and now the Dean Burgon Society to awaken many to the reliability and faithfulness of the King James Bible and its underlying Greek Text.

THE BIBLE
Majestic, eternal, immutable BOOK,
Inspired, inerrant, complete.
The Light of my path as I walk on life's way,
The Guide and the Lamp to my feet.

Its writings are holy and verbally true,
The unalterable Statute of Light,
For profit, for doctrine, for correction, reproof,
Infallible Guide to the right.

My Treasure, my Comfort, my Help, and my Stay,
Incomparable Measure and Rod,
Each page is replete with its textual proof,
The Bible, the exact WORD OF GOD!
By Gertrude Grace Sanborn
(1904--1988)

---

[17] Westcott Brooke Foss, *Some Lessons of the Revised Version of the New Testament*, 1897, p. vi

APPENDIX 1

BAPTIST FELLOWSHIPS AND THE ABANDONMENT OF THE KING JAMES BIBLE

We, the sons of Adam were created to be a sociable people. In the very beginning God said: "*It is not good that the man should be alone.*" (Genesis 2:18) Man needs, desires, and searches for companionship, friendship, and fellowship. We undoubtedly look for such fellowship among those with whom we so often agree. Therefore it follows that, as preachers, we seek to fellowship with those with whom we agree theologically.

The General Association of Regular Baptist Churches (GARBC) was formed in 1932 due to the liberalism and apostasy within the then Northern Baptist Convention. My story is that I grew up within the GARBC and, because of that affiliation, my fellowship was primarily with those within the GARBC. It also followed that because of my GARBC background my initial training for the ministry was in GARB approved schools. After graduation, I pastored a GARB church and then served with a GARB mission board when the GARB still had the approval system. During most of my time within the GARBC it was always the King James Bible that was used, as far as I can remember, from the pulpits of the churches and in the pastors fellowships I attended.

I do remember that when I was a pastor, I received material from a man by the name of Dr. D. A. Waite, who made a big deal about the King James Bible and its underlying Greek Text but I did not really understand the issue and did not take the time to research the issue. When we arrived on the mission field, one of the missionaries we served with eventually abandoned the King James for the NIV in the early 80's. Yet, in my early years of ministry I always used the King James Bible, but it was, however, with no real conviction as to why. A firm heartfelt conviction that the King James Bible is God's Word in English was formed in my heart only after reading Dean John Burgon's, *The Revision Revised*. Oh, how that conviction charged and changed my life and ministry. That heart conviction on the Bible issue affected not only me but affected those with whom I felt comfortable in fellowshipping with as well. This issue on the Bible will separate!!!

During our fourteen years with the GARB mission agency more of the missionaries were changing to other versions. Two of the missionaries in Bangladesh that were heavily involved in translation work were Dr Viggo Olsen, and Lynn Silvernale. In their translation work they also cooperated with the liberal United Bible Societies (UBS). Silvernale wrote the booklet, *By The Word*, in which she praises the work of Eugene Nida and his dynamic equivalency. Silvernale is now with ABWE's translation ministry, WORD Ministries, www.wordmin.com.

Viggo Olsen is retired and living in California, but is still doing translation work. His most recent labour in translation is a *"Muslim-friendly English translation of the Book of Matthew."*[18] The cover to the gospel of Matthew is green with gold lettering. Green has been associated with Islam since the days of the Muslim prophet Muhammad.

Titled '*The Holy Injil*,' their translation of familiar names helps cross the cultural divide with Muslims, as evidenced by this opening passage in Matthew:

> "*This is the record of the family line of 'Isa al-Masih. He is the son of Dawud. He is also the son of Ibrahim. Ibrahim was the father of Ishaq, Ishaq was the father of Ya'qub.*"

Dr. Olsen's team also translates God as 'Allah,' which is controversial in some circles."[19] Think about it--a Muslim friendly Bible! Is there a sinner's friendly Bible? How is the Bible ever seen friendly to a person who is dead in sins and walking "*according to the course of this world, according to the prince of the power of the air, the spirit that now worketh in the children of disobedience*"? It isn't until their spiritual eyes are opened to the truth and they repent of their sins and accept the Lord Jesus Christ as their personal Saviour that the Word of God is seen as their friend!

At the same time that the mission we were with was throwing out the King

---

[18] http://www.assistnews.net/Stories/2012/s12050122.htm

[19] http://www.assistnews.net/Stories/2012/s12050122.htm

James Bible, many of our supporting churches in the GARBC were changing versions as well. This situation made it very uncomfortable for us when we had field council meetings and when we were in the states on furlough reporting back to our churches. Even our home sending church was contemplating changing versions. One time my wife had been back to the States to visit our grown children when she attended a service at our home sending church and the pastor was beginning his work of questioning the King James Bible. He would ask the people in the pew what their translation read. The handwriting was certainly on the wall for, as Amos said in 3:3: *"Can two walk together, except they be agreed?"*

We left the GARBC-approved mission agency, ABWE, in 1994. At the same time, we also resigned from our home sending GARB church. By now, it had also changed Bible versions, so we asked the Lord to give us a church that stood where we did on the Bible issue. Today, we are proudly sent out by the **Bible For Today Baptist Church**.

Sadly, today many more of the GARB churches and missionaries have thrown out the Authorized Version for one of the many new versions. Whereas the choice was once the New International Version (NIV), it is now the English Standard Version (ESV). The church that was our home sending-church for those fourteen years we served with the GARBC mission agency, now has a Detroit Baptist Theological Seminary graduate as pastor. The church exclusively uses the ESV.[20]

Joel R. Grassi says:

> *"At the present time it appears that the ESV is being promoted and accepted by popular Christianity and by many within popular Fundamentalism. A recent (2005) survey among 'young Fundamentalists' found that 14% of those who planned to start a church would do so with the ESV. This is more than three times as many as those who would use the New International Version (NIV) and nearly as many as those who would use the New King James Version (NKJV). This is striking considering that the ESV has only been on the market since 2001. Therefore, a critical analysis*

---

[20] http://www.grandviewparkbaptist.org/about_doctrine.html

of this version is necessary at this time because of the apparent acceptance of the ESV within popular Fundamentalism."[21]

General Association of Regular Baptist Churches – Job Posting

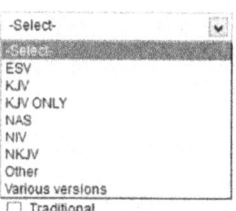

It may be of interest to also know that when a GARB church seeks assistance of the GARB home office in obtaining a pastor, there are cert questions that are asked that were not imaginable or even thought to necessary forty years ago! However, it seems these questions are of associated with the abandonment of the King James Bible! One question is *"dress style for the services."* The answers offered are a smorgasbord to choo from such as *"dressy, business causal, casual, no preference."* Dress standa seem to go down when the King James Bible goes out. A second question is *"worship style."* The answers that are offered are *"blended, contempora hymns/praise choruses, traditional."* The old traditional hymns usually go

---

[21] Joel R. Grassi, A Critical Analysis of the *English Standard Version* of 2001, pdf.,

when the King James Bible is tossed out. Then there is the question as to what version **does the church prefer!**[22]

What Bible one uses, or what a church uses, is it only a preference? How is a church or a fellowship of churches cohesive if a multitude of Bible versions are used? It must be said again that this forsaking of the King James Bible will change the way people dress, the songs a church sings, and the way a church worships God. The King James Bible has been forsaken within the GARBC; but not only in the GARBC, but by other Baptist groups as well. However, this abandonment did not occur in a vacuum and overnight. How did it happen? This leaven spread to the churches through the colleges and seminaries. What really surprised me, as I researched this, is that this disregard for the King James Bible as the most faithful English translation, was promoted in the GARB publications well over fifty years ago and probably earlier.

I was just a junior in high school back in 1961, but that year the GARBC's *Baptist Bulletin* ran several articles entitled "MODERN ENGLISH VERSIONS"[23] by Charles T. Butrin, then an instructor at Omaha Baptist Bible College (now Faith Baptist Bible College) and later Professor of Biblical Studies at Grand Rapids School of Bible and Music. One doesn't have to read far into the first article when they read that:

> "*The American Standard Version is to this day the most faithful literal translation in the English language. The ASV can act as a criterion toward evaluation of any other modern version for the student of the Word who is unfamiliar with Hebrew and Greek.*"

This instructor of students and a writer to a larger audience, the GARBC's *Baptist Bulletin* readers, nowhere in his articles informs his readers that the ASV is translated from a completely different Greek Text than was the King James Bible. Is this being dishonest?

Not having to read much further, Mr Butrin wrote that: "*The ASV is indisputably more accurate than the King James Version. . . .*" The reader immediately knows which English Bible Mr Butrin favours! What

---

[22] http://www.garbc.org/?page_id=9120

[23] http://baptistbulletin.org/?p=653

STANDARD is Mr Butrin comparing the King James Bible and the AV with? Did any of the *Baptist Bulletin* readers question this statement? It would be interesting to know if any did! This was 1961 and the departure was already begun!

Notice, this was in 1961 when professor Butrin wrote these articles for a GARBC audience! On page nine Mr Butrin does tell us that the ASV "*is based on the Westcott and Hort text.*" If he had stopped there one may have accepted this bit of truth, but he goes on to say that:
> "*These two scholars spent a lifetime in the realm of lower criticism to derive a Greek text as close as possible to the original text on the basis of the best manuscripts.*"

This is being DISHONEST with the GARBC *Baptist Bulletin* reader as far as I am concerned. Mr Butrin makes several assumptions for which he is not questioned. As I will state later, John William Burgon believed Westcott and Hort were followers of a German prejudice built upon fabrications. Also who was to say the two manuscripts that Westcott and Hort used primarily were the "*best manuscripts*"? Again I ask why did not the *Baptist Bulletin* Editor put some disclaimer with these articles or put the other side in a future edition?

Butrin should have known better, but in his fourth article he writes that the Revised Standard Version is simply "*. . . a revision of the King James Version, a purging of the archaisms, an employing of contemporary language which would be meaningful to people today.*" Either Mr Butrin did not know what he was talking about, or only parroted what he had been taught, or was just dishonest. The Revised Standard Version was NOT a revision of the King James Bible, but a translation (poor translation at that) from another Greek text!

Mr Butrin was not a lone voice in the GARBC when it came to the RSV. The main initiator in the formation of the GARBC in 1932 was Dr Robert T. Ketcham, who also served as the GARBC National Representative from 1948-1960. In his sermon, "THE UNKNOWN DEPTHS OF SIN," Dr Ketcham used as his text the RSV translation of Romans 7:13 which reads "*That sin may appear exceedingly sinful.*"[24]

---

[24] Robert T. Ketcham, "*WHY WAS CHRIST A CARPENTER*"? Regular Baptist Press, 18 Oakton Boulevard, Des Plaines, IL., 1966, p.103.

This sermon of Dr Ketcham's was printed by the GARBC's Regular Baptist Press (RBP). Did not Dr Ketcham see or know that the RSV was a product of the very liberalism and apostasy that he had separated from?! As far as RBP is concerned:

> "The **GARBC Council of Eighteen** has approved several Bibles for quoting in Regular Baptist Press products, including the following translations: American Standard Version (1901), English Standard Version, Holman Christian Standard Bible, New American Standard Bible, New International Version (1984), New Scofield Reference Bible, and the Amplified Bible. But the Council's approval of translations applies only to the GARBC's publishing division—and should not be mistaken as a mandate to individual churches. Having approved the 1984 edition of the NIV, the Council will now begin to address the advisability of approving the 2011 version."[25]

This article was written by the Editor of RBP September 2, 2011, **but note** the RSV which Dr. Ketchum quoted in a sermon is not one of the translations sanctioned by the Council of Eighteen! Interesting!

This "*flippant*" attitude toward Bible versions is seen on page 27 of the June, 1961, *Baptist Bulletin* where Mr Butrin wrote in his fourth article "Which Modern Version is Best?"

> "*This was the question that I posed to several **pastors of our GARBC fellowship**. Three of them were partial to The Amplified New Testament, one liked Wuest's Expanded Translation, another preferred the RSV along with the Greek. One liked the Philips and two others were partial to Williams'. It is amusing to observe that some strongly opposed to using one of the liberal versions, while **others, though just as vigorously opposed to liberal theology, did not hesitate to use a liberal translation**, along with a Greek New Testament (Emphasis added).*"

Before going further, please note at least three things in the above article. **First,**

---

[25] http://baptistbulletin.org/?p=18067

this was a question posed to GARBC pastors in 1961! Only someone who was already confident that their question would not stir strife would ask such a question. Mr Butrin knew these pastors had already been duped by their teachers and swallowed the bias toward the new versions, the Critical Greek Text and had a bias against the King James Bible. **Secondly** even though they may have opposed liberal theology they were not hesitate to use the liberals' translation! One would have thought that a pastor would have had enough discernment to KNOW that a liberal translator's product would be biassed to liberal theology! **Thirdly** one can only guess what Greek New Testament a pastor in this group would use! Most assuredly they attended a school where the Critical Greek New Testament was used! This in 1961!

In the same article, Butrin writes saying that The New English Bible and the Revised Standard Version have both "*taken advantage of the latest manuscript discoveries, critical apparati of the lower critics. . . .*" But were the Revised Standard and The New English Bible translated by "*lower critics*"? Dr Thomas Strouse says;

> "*the role of Textual Criticism is to restore or reconstruct a Bible text that God apparently chose not to preserve. This view begs the question as to how the critic will know that the text is restored or reconstructed since the Lord apparently left no exemplar for comparison! The anti-supernatural German rationalistic movement (17th-19th centuries) known as Biblical Criticism spawned several literary-critical fields, one of which was Textual Criticism. The picking and choosing of Bible texts is not Textual Criticism. Textual Criticism is a sophisticated system based on elaborate and evolutionary schemes following human logic to determine the possible origin of variants. The so-called science of Textual riticism is only needed when one believes that God has not accomplished His promise to preserve the inspired original Hebrew, Aramaic, and Greek Words of the autographa.*"[26]

In fact, Dr Thomas Strouse says: "*Since the text of Scripture was never lost, the*

---

[26] Dr. Thomas M. Strouse, *Scholarly Myths Perpetuated on Rejecting the Masoretic Text of OT*, p. 12.

Lord never used textual critics to restore His text."[27]

Mr Butrin did not have much good to say concerning the King James Bible in his four articles. On page eight of the first article he wrote almost despondently that: *"the KJV has become so endeared to the English-speaking world that many Christians are reluctant to substitute any other version for it."* Oh, yes, Mr Butrin continues to tell us: *"a problem arises here. Because we no longer use Elizabethan English, youngsters find it increasingly hard to understand the many archaic expressions of the KJV."* All of this is said against the King James Bible with no comment made by the *Bulletin's* Editor in Defense of the King James Bible or its underlying Greek text. No wonder the GARBC eventually tossed the King James Bible aside when the GARBC's *Baptist Bulletin* and the GARBC-approved schools walked hand in hand in the overthrowing of the King James Bible!

These articles by Professor Butrin did not go unnoticed for those who were later taught in the school of Westcott and Hort's German rationalism. Butrin's articles prompted Central Seminary's Jeff Straub to write fifty years later that Butrin:

> "... noted that some of the versions held a liberal bias, but he did not dismiss the use of modern versions out of hand, nor did he show the undue deference for the KJV that would later characterize a hyper-fundamentalist wing of the movement. This non-KJV-only view has continued to be the normative position of the GARBC as a fellowship, despite some of its individual pastors who have dissented."[28]

I agree that, as an association. the GARBC has never stated a position in favour of the King James Bible or any other English translation. Nevertheless, I personally would have never sensed such dislike for the King James Bible while attending any GARB church in Iowa in the 1960's. My research in discovering what Mr Butrin wrote back in 1961 was a shock to me. If the official publication of the GARBC would print articles like Mr Butrin's in 1961, it isn't any surprise how the GARBC has today almost completely

---

Ibid., p. 13

Jeff Struab, *Fundamentalism and the King James Version: How a Venerable English Translation Became a Litmus Test for Orthodoxy*, SBJT 15.4 (2011): 44-63.

displaced the King James Bible from its pulpits and schools.

Again, I ask, how did the GARB churches, schools, and mission agencies come to the place where the King James Bible has been openly replaced with other English versions? From this paper, it did not happen overnight. The reality is that it has taken place through years of training preachers in schools using the German rationalistic Critical Text in the Greek classes without question but then continuing to use the King James Bible in the other Bible classes. Where the two differ, the Critical Text is favoured above the reading of the King James Bible. This duplicity is then played out in the churches where these preachers are called to preach the Word. However, the preacher will so often use the King James Bible in the pulpit, but undermine its authority by stating *"the Greek text reads"* (meaning the Critical Greek text) or *"it would be better translated"* or *"the better manuscripts say"* or *"the ESV renders it."* These statements cause doubt in the minds of the person in the pew, and eventually the King James Bible is abandoned for a new version.

Dean John William Burgon saw the ultimate abandonment of the Textus Receptus and the Authorised Version if the German rationalists were to be followed. He wrote in a footnote in *The Revision Revised* that: **"Men must begin by unlearning the *German prejudices of the last fifty years*...."**[29] The Dean went on to say that the New Greek Text of Westcott and Hort was: *"Built up on a fallacy which since 1831 has been dominant in Germany . . . "*[30] John Burgon saw that the Westcott and Hort's New Greek Text was a composition *". . . of those wretched fabrications which are just now in favour with the German school . . . "*[31]

This love for German rationalism John Burgon said began:
> *"in A.D. 1831, under the auspices of Dr. Lachmann, 'a new departure' is made. Up springs what may be called the new German school of Textual Criticism,—of which the*

---

[29] John William Burgon, *Revision Revised*, pdf., *The Project Gutenberg EBook of The Revision Revised*, p. 50.

[30] Ibid., p. 249

[31] John William Burgon, *Revision Revised*, pdf., *The Project Gutenberg EBook of The Revision Revised*, p. 259

fundamental principle is a superstitious deference to the decrees of cod. B."

Sadly, the Dean went on to say: *"The heresy prevails for fifty years (1831-81) and obtains many adherents."*[32]

Those *"adherents"* make up the majority of the teachers in the schools from which the GARBC obtains its preachers. Those schools are: Bob Jones University, Central Baptist Theological Seminary, Faith Baptist Bible College and Seminary, Baptist Bible College and Seminary, Clarks Summit, Pa., Detroit Baptist Theological Seminary, and Calvary Baptist Theological Seminary, Lansdale, PA.

As to textual criticism, John Burgon spoke of two schools which he said:
"it cannot be too plainly stated that no compromise is possible between our respective methods,—yours and mine: between the NEW GERMAN system in its most aggravated and in fact intolerable form, to which you have incautiously and unconditionally given in your adhesion; and the OLD ENGLISH school of Textual Criticism, of which I humbly avow myself a disciple."[33]

It is the *"intolerable"* German system that Westcott, Hort, and their followers have adopted! That system has leavened every new English translation. This is all due to the fact that the new English translations are a child of Westcott and Hort's Greek Text.

However, not only have the new versions used a Greek text based on the *"intolerable"* German system, but they have used a different Old Testament text as well. The ESV seems to be the choice of many GARB churches. The ESV translators say:
"The ESV is based on the Masoretic text of the Hebrew Bible as found in Biblia Hebraica Stuttgartensia (2nd ed., 1983), and on the Greek text in the 1993 editions of the Greek New Testament (4th corrected ed.), published by the United Bible

---

Ibid., p. 309

John William Burgon, *Revision Revised*, pdf., *The Project Gutenberg EBook of The Revision Revised*, p. 529

Societies (UBS), and Novum Testamentum Graece (27th ed.), edited by Nestle and Aland."[34]

Dr. D. A. Waite tells us:
"*the Old Testament basis of our KING JAMES BIBLE is the traditional Masoretic Hebrew text, the 2nd **Rabbinic Bible, Daniel Bomberg Edition, edited by Ben Chayyim** in 1524-25. It was called the First Rabbinic Bible. During this time they came up with a standard Masoretic Hebrew Old Testament text and it lasted 400 years. That standard was used even in Kittel's first two editions, 1906 and 1912.*"[35]

The Old Testament text that the ESV translators used is:
"*a revision of the third edition of the Biblia Hebraica edited by Rudolf Kittel, the first Bible to be based on the **Leningrad Codex*** (Emphasis added). *The Leningrad Codex is the oldest complete Hebrew Bible still preserved. It originally appeared in installments, from 1968 to 1976, with the first one-volume edition in 1977; it has since been reprinted many times. The text is a nearly exact copy of the Masoretic Text as recorded in the*

Leningrad Codex. The Masoretic notes are completely revised."[36]

NOTE the ESV used the "*third edition*" of Kittel's.

Dr. Waite says the Hebrew Old Testament edition that he:
"*used when . . . a student of Dr. Merrill F. Unger at Dallas Theological Seminary (1948-53), was the 1937 edition of the Biblia Hebraica by Kittel. All of a sudden, in 1937, Kittel changed his Hebrew edition and followed what they called the **Ben Asher Masoretic Text** instead of the **Ben Chayyim**.*

---

[34] http://www.esv.org/esv/translation/about/

[35] D. A. Waite, DEFENDING THE KING JAMES BIBLE, The Bible For Today, INC., 900 Pa Avenue, Collingswood, NJ 08108, p. 38.

[36] http://pdfcast.org/paid/9781598561630

Dean John Burgon's Defense of the Authorized Version 49

> They followed, in that text, the **Leningrad Manuscript,** *(B19a or 'L'). The date on it was 1008AD."*[37]

Dr. Waite then writes, on page 29, about an experience he had when the class he attended at Dallas was:

> "*reading in the book of Isaiah, using the Kittle Bible (Biblia Hebraica by Rudolf Kittel) and of course it has all these footnotes. Dr. Unger read the word in a way different from the Masoretic text. He used one of the footnotes as a basis for the change. I raised my hand and said, 'Dr. Unger, why did you change this text?' He replied, 'It just reads better that way.' That is because down in the footnotes, every time they want to change it, with no evidence whatever, the footnotes read 'L' which stands for the Latin word legendum. It means 'which read.' This 'L' appears in Genesis 1:9 and after the 'L.'*

Dr. Waite tells us it said '*probably this.*' In other words, there's no evidence, no document. It is just conjecture and guesswork."[38]

The Hebrew texts which the ASV, NIV, NASV, and ESV use, all part company from that Hebrew text underlying the King James Bible. Dr. Waite gives his personal opinion of the Hebrew text underlying the ESV, ASV, NIV, and NASV saying the Biblia Hebraica of Kittel or Stuttgartensia "*are false Hebrew texts which are improper bases for the Hebrew Old Testament.*"[39]

The translators of the ESV say without apology that "*the 1971 RSV text*" provided "*the starting point for our work.*"[40] The RSV has a copyright by the liberal apostate National Council of Churches. That should throw up a red flag. It was:

> "*In 1971, the RSV Bible was re-released with the Second Edition of the Translation of the New Testament. Whereas in*

D. A. Waite, *DEFENDING THE KING JAMES BIBLE*, The Bible For Today, INC., 900 Park Avenue, Collingswood, NJ 08108, p. 27.

D. A. Waite, *DEFENDING THE KING JAMES BIBLE*, The Bible For Today, INC., 900 Park Avenue, Collingswood, NJ 08108, p. 30.

Ibid., p. 31

http://www.esv.org/esv/translation/about/

1962 the translation panel had merely authorized a handful of changes, in 1971 they gave the New Testament text a thorough editing. This Second Edition incorporated Greek manuscripts not previously available to the RSV translation panel, namely, the Bodmer Papyri, published in 1956-61. The most obvious changes were the restoration of Mark 16.9-20 (the long ending) and John 7.53-8.11 (in which Jesus forgives an adulteress) to the text (in 1946, they were put in footnotes). Also restored was Luke 22.19b-20, containing the bulk of Jesus' institution of the Lord's Supper. In the 1946-52 text, this had been cut off at the phrase 'This is my body', and the rest had only been footnoted, since this verse did not appear in the original Codex Bezae manuscript used by the translation committee. The description of Christ's ascension in Luke 24:51 had the footnote '. . . and was carried up into heaven' restored to the text. Luke 22.43-44, which had been part of the text in 1946-52, was relegated to the footnote section because of its questionable authenticity; in these verses an angel appears to Jesus in Gethsemane to strengthen and encourage Him before His arrest and crucifixion. Many other verses were rephrased or rewritten for greater clarity and accuracy. Moreover, the footnotes concerning monetary values were no longer expressed in terms of dollars and cents but in terms of how long it took to earn each coin (the denarius was no longer defined as twenty cents but as a day's wage). The book of Revelation, called 'The Revelation to John' in the previous editions, was retitled 'The Revelation to John (The Apocalypse)'. Some of these changes to the RSV New Testament had already been introduced in the 1965-66 Catholic Edition, and their

introduction into the Protestant edition was done to pave the way for the publication of the RSV Common Bible in 1973."[41]

---

[41] http://en.wikipedia.org/wiki/Revised_Standard_Version#19 Second Edition of the New Testament

In the ESV:

> "... *after giving the legal requirements for citing, quoting, or printing excerpts of the ESV, makes the following statement: 'The Holy Bible, English Standard Version (ESV) is adapted from the Revised Standard Version of the Bible, copyright Division of Christian Education of the National Council of the Churches of Christ in the U.S.A. All rights reserved.'"*[42]

The RSV was a very ecumenical version as:

> "*The Revised Standard Version Bible Committee is a continuing body, comprising about thirty members, both men and women. **Ecumenical in representation, it includes scholars affiliated with various Protestant denominations, as well as several Roman Catholic members** (Emphasis and underlining added), an Eastern Orthodox member, and a Jewish member who serves in the Old Testament section.*"[43]

Whereas, the 1952 RSV was rejected by fundamentalists; but, with a little tweeking of the text, fundamentalists have accepted the ESV which admits its heritage is based on the RSV. Since the ESV follows so closely the 1971 RSV one could interpret the "E" representing Ecumenical in place of English.

Before I close, I believe another reason so many preachers get in the version changing business is due to their following "big name" preachers. Most, if not all of the "big name" preachers, agree with the professors in the schools that teach the Critical Greek text as the best to the less known preachers. One such "big name" preacher to many GARBC is John MacArthur. MacArthur is a follower and promoter of the Critical Greek text. This is seen for example in his sermon entitled "*The Fitting End to Mark's Gospel.*" It is quite lengthy so only a portion will be quoted here. MacArthur says:

> "*What you hold in your hand right now, your Bible, I can tell you is an accurate, English translation of the original manuscripts written by the authors of the Bible. It is accurate. If I didn't believe that we had an accurate*

---

[42] Joel R. Grassi, *A Critical Analysis of the English Standard Version of 2001*, pdf., p. 5

[43] http://www.ncccusa.org/newbtu/reader.html

translation of the original text of Holy Scripture, why would I endeavor to explain it verse-by-verse and word-by word? It's very, very essential and very foundational to understand that what you have in your hand in a twentieth century, if you had the NAS, or twenty-first century if you have the ESV, English translation is an accurate translation of texts that originated thousands of years ago. And the reason that I can say that is true is because I understand the science and the history of manuscripts and the passing down of Holy Scripture. That is one of the most important things you learn in seminary because if you have any wavering in your confidence about the integrity of your translation of the Bible, it will suck the conviction right out of your heart. That is why those who attack the truth, attack first the veracity of Scripture. Because if the Bible can be shown to be inaccurate, or an inadequate translation, or wrong, then we have no assurance of anything."

"Now that leads me to have you turn to the book of Mark because here somebody might say, 'That issue of accuracy is called into question.' Because there is this odd ending of Mark, starting in verse 9 and running down to verse 20, you see a section in brackets, a bracket before the word 'now' in verse 9, and a bracket after the word 'followed' in verse 20. And if you have a New American Standard, or an English Standard Version, even if you have a New King James Version, there will be a note in the margin explaining that this is a variant, this is a text that has been added to Mark. That is a most providential way to end our 43-year study because now that you have 43 years, those of you who have endured it all, 43 years of absolute unshakable confidence in the veracity of Scripture, we can talk about the science of it."

"Nothing . . . nothing in ancient literature, even comes close to the mass of manuscripts that we have on the New Testament. And what they demonstrate is the uniformity and the consistency. There are, as I said, twenty-five thousand ancient manuscripts. There are five thousand, six hundred or so Greek manuscripts and they go way back. We have Greek manuscripts from the second century, from the third century.

Dean John Burgon's Defense of the Authorized Version 53

Our Lord lived in the first century. There is a manuscript called P-52 and they're numbered and named according to the people who found them, or the location, or something like that. This one called P-52 has parts of the gospel of John and it dates from 100 to 150 and John was living in the nineties. Somebody copied an original, most likely, or a copy of an original, very near the original.

There is another papyrus, they were writing on papyrus so they're called papyri, there's another one called the Bodmer Papyri in which we find John and Luke and it dates from 175 to 225. And then there's the very famous papyrus called the Chester Beatty papyrus that has all four gospels and the book of Acts and it dates around 200. They go way back.

Here's the amazing part. There probably shouldn't be a lot of manuscripts from those early years. Why? Because second century in particular and the third century, for sure, was a time of immense Christian persecution, and an effort to stamp out Christianity by the destruction of Christians and Christian scriptures. But the Lord preserved these ancient texts, copies of those very close to the original.

Once you get into the fourth century, around 325, or so, you get Constantine making Christianity legal. The persecution ends and now manuscripts proliferate. They're everywhere. And so by the time you pass say 325, the Council of Nicea, we begin to see manuscripts in abundance.

The two most important ones, one is called, it's a Codex, this is called a Codex because it is a bound volume, rather than a scroll. The first one that is very important is called Sinaiticus and it's about 350 and it's the whole New Testament. The second important one is called Vaticanus, 325 and it's the whole Bible. By the way, both Sinaiticus and Vaticanus end Mark at verse 8.

We also have eight thousand ancient copies of the New Testament in Latin called the Vulgate. And the Vulgate dates from 382 to 405. We also have 350-plus copies of the Bible in Syriac that goes back to the 200's. If I'm belaboring this a little bit, I'm going to tell you why. We have all these ancient manuscripts that when compared all say the same thing. The early church fathers, for example, before 325 because there was the Council of Nicea in 325, they're called the ante Nicene fathers because they were before Nicea, the early fathers in the 200's and 300's, if you just read... here were these guys writing all kinds of theology, and all kinds of biblical study material, if you take the church fathers prior to 325, there are among those fathers about 32 thousand quotes from the New Testament. There are so many quotes from the New Testament among those fathers in the writings of the fathers, which we have, which are held in libraries, that we can reconstruct the complete New Testament from nothing but the writings of the fathers. That's another source to find what the New Testament said in ancient times.

The writings of the early church fathers also confirm the accuracy of the gospels. There are over nineteen thousand quotations from the gospels in the writings of the fathers. So whether you're reading a Greek manuscript, a Syriac Bible, or whether you're looking at a Latin Vulgate or whether you're reading a quote from a church father, it is crystal clear that they all had the same thing. They would be reading essentially in their language what you're reading today in yours because yours is drawn from those ancient manuscripts."

"By the way, we have all kinds of manuscript evidence to know that was added later. I told you the two most important manuscripts, Sinaiticus and Vaticanus both end at verse 8, as do the other ancient manuscripts. Our translations are based on the most ancient Greek manuscripts. And they don't have that short ending, and they certainly don't have that long ending, verses 9 through 20.

In the fourth century, for example, two of the fathers, Eusebius and Jerome, wrote that almost all Greek manuscripts of the New Testament end at verse 8. Did they know those other endings existed? Yes they did. They knew they existed. In the second century, Justin Martyr and Tatian knew about other endings. Irenaeus, also, Irenaeus is in 150 to 200, he knows about this long ending because he quotes *verse 19 from it. They knew these endings existed. They existed early. But even by the fourth century, Eusebius says, "The Greek manuscripts do not include these endings . . . the originals."*

Now if you happen to have a King James Bible, or a New King James, you will find verses 9 to 20 in the regular flow of text without brackets because the King James and the New King James are based on a medieval text . . . a medieval text, based on later texts. However, since that time, we have discovered the earlier texts, so all the later translations, NAS, NAS Update, ESV, NIV, etc., etc., are all based on the more ancient texts. That's why if you have any of those, it's bracketed; because the earlier texts omitted it.

The external evidence indicates that this doesn't belong and it's pretty good evidence. There are some other endings floating around too, by the way, some others that you don't need to know about. So we would say external evidence argues for exclusion, not inclusion. And that would pretty much cross the board with textual scholars."[44]

Here we have John MacArthur saying he and his people "*absolute unshakable confidence in the veracity of Scripture*" and yet he tells his people that:

"*if you happen to have a King James Bible, or a New King James, you will find verses 9 to 20 in the regular flow of text without brackets because the King James and the New King James are based on a medieval text . . . a medieval text, based on later texts. However, since that time, we have discovered the earlier texts . . .*"

So you can trust the newer versions he mentions but not the King James or New King James. Whatever!

John MacArthur pretty much regurgitates what the critical Greek text professors in the schools (including MacArthur's Master's Seminary) teach, but because MacArthur is such a prolific writer, well known in evangelical circles,

---

[44] http://www.gty.org/resources/sermons/41-85

and has the Master's Seminary, what he says sticks with many as truth. If John MacArthur says it is so, it must be true!

So what may one determine from the history just given concerning the GARBC on the Bible issue?

1. What has taken place within the GARBC concerning the King James Bible is occurring, will occur or has already occurred in other independent Baptist fellowships and associations as well.

2. The removal or the undermining of the King James Bible in GARB churches began not long after the GARBC was formed.

3. Initially, when the GARBC leaders separated from the liberalism and apostasy of the Northern Baptist Convention, these men did not totally forsake the Northen Baptists Convention's "intolerable" German rationalistic textual criticism.

4. This "intolerable" German rationalistic textual criticism and its ever changing Greek text was brought over and used in the GARBC approved schools.

5. The preachers, trained in the GARBC schools, accepted this "intolerable" German textual criticism and its ever changing Greek text, then carried it into the pulpits of the GARB churches.

6. Through the preachers the churches finally tossed out the King James Bible to accept one of the new versions based on the "intolerable" German textual criticism's ever changing Greek text.

7. By throwing out the King James Bible for a new version, the churches also adapted themselves to new ways of dress, songs, and worship.

8. Not taking a solid, positive position on the King James Bible issue, several things occurred.

One, the GARBC saw its approved schools go the way of new evangelicalism in not only accepting a multitude of new versions, but also dropping the name Baptist, and weakening their standard of dress and music. The GARBC approval system *"was meant to facilitate the rapid severing of ties if an institution went bad."* Since approval was merely an executive recommendation, it could be withdrawn quickly and (it was thought) painlessly. In the early years, the GARBC actually did approve and quickly disapprove a variety of agencies. Furthermore, a variety of agencies sought approval only to drop it later on.

For decades it seemed as if the GARBC had hit upon the ideal compromise between the associational model and the service organization model. When Los Angeles Baptist Seminary strayed into a bit of Pentecostalism, approval was withdrawn until the aberrant theology could be purged. When Wheaton College agreed to fund a chair of Regular Baptist Theology, it was approved—for one year, until the plan proved unworkable.

Over time, however, the approved agencies came to be regarded (at least popularly) as the property of the association. The Council of 18 became very reluctant to pull the plug on any institution. Loyalty shifted toward the agencies, and the result was a de facto return to the associational principle in its most obnoxious form. For a time during the 1990s, the GARBC began to resemble a convention.

One reason for this was that the visibility of the agencies gave them a disproportionate amount of influence over the business of the association. Agency presidents and representatives became popular speakers who occupied many platforms in the course of a year. Given their exposure, they were easily elected to the Council of 18, where they became the individuals who were approving their own institutions.

> "*By the 1980s, it was becoming apparent that some of the agencies no longer advocated the historic position of the GARBC.* Even though the bond between association and agencies was supposed to be loose, it still provided something of *an umbilical cord through which theological and methodological infection was transmitted from those agencies to the churches.*
>
> During the 1980s, conservatives within the GARBC attempted to address some of these issues, but the balance of loyalty lay with the agencies. A 1990 proposal to keep agency executives from approving their own schools met a resounding defeat. The balance of sentiment began to shift, however, as the agendas of some institutions became more publicly visible. The approval system was finally dropped in 2000 (Emphasis added)."[45]

---

[45] http://seminary.wcts1030.com/publications/Nick/Nick170.html

Note, it is said that the *"theological and methodological infection was transmitted from those agencies to the churches."* THE AGENCIES LEAVEN THE CHURCHES! This leaven is a bias against the King James Bible and its underlying Greek text!

This bias affected those areas mentioned earlier. For instance Grand Rapids Baptist College is now Cornerstone University and it claims to be **"Multi-denominational"** with **"more than 45 denominations represented"**[46].

Not only have the schools dropped the name Baptist but so have many of the GARB churches. For instance:

> *"At their November 2011 meeting, the Council of Eighteen approved a new policy stating that a GARBC church 'must publicly identify itself as a Baptist church in its corporate documents and in its practice.' In essence, the new policy allows churches to remain in fellowship with the GARBC even if Baptist is not in their published name. The policy retains our historic emphasis on the way a church functions. These churches will continue to be identified parenthetically as 'a Baptist church' in our GARBC directory."*[47]

I wonder if any of the initial leaders of the GARBC ever thought a church would desire to associate with a Baptist group and not have Baptist in its name!?

Cedarville University was a GARBC approved school until the system was dropped and it is now an approved school of the Southern Baptist Convention. The **music** at Cedarville is CCM and the university often hosts such CCM personalities such as Paul Baloche. Baloche is one of the worship pastors at:

> *"the non-denominational Community Fellowship in Lindale, Texas which also has Awana. Awana is a another book! Baloche has co- written songs with Matt Redman, Brenton Brown, Tim Hughes, Chris Tomlin and others. He is by no means a separatist. He has also participated in the Saddleback worship and music conference. At the Saddleback worship and music conference in 2009 Baloche*

---

[46] http://www.cornerstone.edu/quick-facts

[47] http://baptistbulletin.org/?p=27236

and friends are singing the Beatles' Twist & Shout. It has the dressed down look and the noise but no lights as it was filmed during the day. Has it sunk in yet that CCM is a mixed multitude going back into Egypt!?"[48]

Now, this is not to say every church that uses the King James Bible is immune to the use of CCM or is it to say it is not weak in its practice of ecclesiastical separation. However, it is to say that a weak position on the Bible issue will all too often lead a church in these other directions.

Western Baptist College in Oregon was once an approved school of the GARBC, but it too has dropped the name Baptist to become Corban University. It also today is an approved school of the Southern Baptist Convention.

So this is where we find many of our fundamentalist brethren. However, we must remember the Dean Burgon Society definitely has a place in today's world and there are several things which we as a society can do. **The first thing** we can do is to be kind, but firm, in our stand for the Defense of the King James Bible and its underlying Greek Text. **Secondly**, continue this annual conference as an encouragement to us, but also a place where others may attend to obtain information not heard anywhere else. **Thirdly**, pray for openings for our DBS members to speak in Christian colleges and Universities on the text issue. **Fourthly**, disseminate literature wherever we can. **Fifthly**, write on your blog and website concerning this Bible issue. It is surprising how many people come across these sites and will read what you have written. **Lastly**, ask the Lord to keep each one of us true to His Words, and the issue before us. I remember, not long after I joined the DBS, a follower of Ruckman (Gary Hudson) came the DBS way and spoke at one of the annual meetings. It wasn't long before he left us and went to the Critical text crowd and became one of our enemies. He now writes or has written articles that have appeared on the internet against the DBS and the King James Bible. Sadly, that will happen, but may it not happen with one of us.

David C. Bennett, *CCM IS NOT THE PROBLEM*, The Bible For Today Press, 900 Park venue, Collingswood, NJ 08108, p.34.

APPENDIX 2

THE ENGLISH STANDARD VERSION 2011

Allow me to give just a little of my background which may explain why I am writing this review. My association with the General Association of Regular Baptist Churches (GARBC) extended over many decades. My undergraduate work was done in a GARBC approved school where one professor used the ASV while the others used the King James Bible and the Critical Greek text was used in the Greek class.

We still have one supporting church affiliated with the GARBC. It is the church I was saved in and this church continues to use the King James Bible. However, as I said in Appendix 1, many GARB churches have steadily moved away from the King James Bible, primarily due to the teaching the pastors have received in the schools.

As an association, the GARBC's Council of Eighteen officially endorsed several versions of the Scriptures in September, 2011. The men comprising this council:

> "*approved several Bibles for quoting in Regular Baptist Press products, including the following translations: American Standard Version (1901),* **English Standard Version***, Holman Christian Standard Bible, New American Standard Bible, New International Version (1984), New Scofield Reference Bible, and the Amplified Bible. But the Council's approval of translations applies only to the GARBC's publishing division—and should not be mistaken as a mandate to individual churches. Having approved the 1984 edition of the NIV, the Council will now begin to address the advisability of approving the 2011 version.*"[49]

The English Standard Version (ESV) is mentioned in the above article but, in fact, it was:

---

[49] http://baptistbulletin.org/?p=18067

"*In 2009 The GARBC Council of Eighteen added the ESV to the list of translations approved for authors to use in Regular Baptist Press publications. When the council began the policy in 1963, the list included the KJV, ASV, Berkeley Version, and Williams translation. This list was expanded through the years and now includes ASV, ESV, Holman Christian Standard Bible, NASB, NIV, New Scofield Bible, and Amplified Bible.*"[50]

This is quite a list that the GARB's Council of Eighteen have endorsed for use in the GARB's publishing arm, Regular Baptist Press (RBP). Each version reads different from the other, but, in spite of those differences exhibited among these versions, the GARBC *Baptist Bulletin* would tell its readers that "*believers can be assured that their English Bible is an accurate translation.*"[51] This belief allows the writers for RBP to do like the professors in the colleges. For instance in the "CHOOSING TO BE SPIRITUAL" adult study, the authors comment on 1 Corinthians 3 verses 1 and 3 saying:

"*In 1 Corinthians 3:1 the Greek word for 'carnal' is sarkinos. It means 'flesh' and emphasizes the idea of weakness. In 3:3 the term for 'carnal' is sarkikos. It means 'fleshly' and emphasizes the idea of wilfulness.*"[52]

Here the authors do not tell the student they are using the King James Bible as their English text but using the Critical text to explain the Greek words. The Critical text does change, as they said, BUT the text underlying our King James Bible uses the same Greek word in both places! Is this being deceitful on purpose? I asked the then RBP editor, Vernon Miller, about this when he was in Sydney. He said I was being too picky. Too picky?! If I were to use the NIV or ESV as the English text and criticize it using the Textus Receptus would Mr. Miller think I was being dishonest or would he care? I don't know, but I know what I think!

No wonder people and churches are not stable when it comes to what English

---

[50] http://baptistbulletin.org/?p=16799

[51] *Ibid.*

[52] Dave and Pat Warren, *Choosing to Be Spiritual*, Regular Baptist Press, 1300 North Meach Road, Schaumburg, IL, 60173-4888, p. 7.

version they use. Most do not think anything about changing versions whenever a new one comes on the market. One of the very popular versions within fundamentalism and conservatives today is the ESV.

The ESV Translating Committee

One university professor wrote that:
> "The English Standard Version was published by some fundamentalist and ultra-conservative Christian scholars who were dissatisfied with the inaccuracies of the New International Version . . . and other dynamic/functional equivalency translations, but also unhappy with the excessive literalism of the NASB. Their solution was to revise the RSV, which they mostly liked since it was fairly literal and in the KJV stylistic tradition, but 'correct' the places where an accurate translation of the Hebrew and Greek had made the RSV unpopular with many conservative Christians."[53]

Note the above writer said *"The English Standard Version was published by some fundamentalist and ultra-conservative Christian scholars. . . ."* How can the ESV be the product of fundamentalist and ultra-conservative Christian scholars when they *"come from twelve countries and more than twenty denominations."*[54] How many denominations can you think of that you consider truly *"fundamental"* or *"ultra-conservative"*?

It is said the ESV translators make up a:
> *"100-member team, which is international and represents many denominations, shares a commitment to historic evangelical orthodoxy, and to the authority and sufficiency of the inerrant Scriptures."*[55]

"Many denominations"!

Here are those who *"comprise the team of more than fifty Translation Review Scholars who completed their work when the ESV was first published in 2001.*[56]

---

[53] http://courses.missouristate.edu/markgiven/rel102/bt.htm

[54] http://www.esv.org/esv/scholarship/trusted-scholarship/

[55] *Ibid.*

[56] http://www.esv.org/esv/scholarship/translation-review-scholars/

See if you can find anyone who would claim to be a fundamentalist in this group!

Dr. T. D. Alexander, Director of the Christian Training Centre, Union Theological College, Belfast

Dr. Clinton E. Arnold, Professor of New Testament Language and Literature, Talbot School of Theology

Dr. David W. Baker, Professor of Old Testament and Semitic Languages, Ashland Theological Seminary

Dr. William D. Barrick, Professor of Old Testament, The Master's Seminary *(Dr Barrick "served with the Association of Baptists for World Evangelism (ABWE)"[57] before joining the faculty at the Master's Seminary 1997. Dr Barrick served in Bangladesh with ABWE as a translator. The ABWE Bengali translation of the Scriptures was very fluid to say the least. I personally would not trust a version that was a result Dr Barrick 's review. I believe Dr. Barrick would claim to be "conservative" but NEVER a fundamentalist! Now that is my own opinion!)* Dr. Hans F. Bayer, Associate Professor of New Testament, Covenant Seminary

Dr. Gregory Beale, Professor of New Testament, Wheaton College

Dr. Ronald Bergey, Professeur d'Hébreu et d'Ancient Testament, Faculté libre de Théologie réformée, Aix-en-Provence, France

Dr. Daniel I. Block, John R. Sampey Professor of Old Testament Interpretation, The Southern Baptist Theological Seminary

Dr. Craig L. Blomberg, Professor of New Testament, Denver Seminary

Dr. Darrell L. Bock, Research Professor of New Testament Studies, Dallas Theological Seminary

Dr. Irvin A. Busenitz, Vice President for Academic Administration, Professor of Bible Exposition and Old Testament, The Master's Seminary

Mr. Edward H. Chandler, Ph.D. (cand.), Catholic University of America

Dr. Daniel L. Gard, Dean of Graduate Studies, Concordia Theological Seminary, Fort Wayne, IN

Dr. Robert P. Gordon, Regius Professor of Hebrew, Cambridge University

Dr. Gene L. Green, Associate Professor of New Testament, Wheaton College

Dr. Michael Grisanti, Associate Professor of Old Testament, The Master's Seminary

---

[57] http://www.tms.edu/FacultyIntroduction.aspx?FacultyID=8

Dr. George H. Guthrie, Associate Professor of Christian Studies, Union University
Dr. Scott J. Hafemann, Professor, Hawthorne Chair of New Testament Greek and Exegesis, Wheaton College
Dr. Charles D. Harvey, Visiting Assistant Professor of Biblical Studies, Taylor University
Dr. Richard S. Hess, Professor of Old Testament, Denver Seminary
Dr. Harold W. Hoehner, Senior Professor of New Testament Studies, Dallas Theological Seminary
Dr. David M. Howard, Jr. Professor of Old Testament and Hebrew, New Orleans Baptist Theological Seminary
Dr. Gordon P. Hugenberger, Senior Pastor, Park Street Church, Boston, MA
Dr. Philip Johnston, Professor of Old Testament, Wycliff Hall, UK
Dr. Reggie McReynolds Kidd, Associate Professor of New Testament, Reformed Theological Seminary, Orlando, FL
Dr. Nobuyoshi Kiuchi, Professor of Old Testament, Tokyo Christian University
Dr. Andreas J. Köstenberger, Associate Professor of New Testament, Southeastern Baptist Theological Seminary
Dr. V. Philips Long, Professor of Old Testament, Regent College
Dr. Ernest Lucas, Professor of Old Testament, Bristol Baptist College
Dr. Dennis R. Magary, Associate Professor of Old Testament and Semitic Languages, Trinity Evangelical Divinity School
Dr. Walter A. Maier, III., Professor of Old Testament, Concordia Theological Seminary, Fort Wayne, IN
Dr. J. Gordon McConville, Professor of Old Testament, Cheltenham and Gloucester College of Higher Education
Dr. Christopher Mitchell, Theological Editor, Concordia Publishing House
Dr. Leon Morris, Former Principal of Ridley College, Melbourne, Australia
Dr. Russell Nelson, Professor of Religious Studies, Division Chair, Concordia University College of Alberta
Dr. Raymond Ortlund, Jr., Pastor, First Presbyterian Church, Augusta, GA
Dr. Douglas A. Oss, Pastor, Capital Christian Center, Salt Lake City, UT
Dr. John N. Oswalt, Research Professor of Old Testament, Wesley Biblical Seminary

Dr. Iain Provan, Marshall Sheppard Professor of Biblical Studies, Regent College
Dr. Paul R. Raabe, Professor of Exegetical Theology, Concordia Seminary, St. Louis, MO
Dr. Thomas Renz, Professor of Old Testament, Oak Hill Theological College-London, UK
Mr. Max Rogland, Ph.D. (cand.) Leiden University
Dr. Allen Ross, Former Professor of Old Testament, Trinity Episcopal School for Ministry
Dr. Thomas R. Schreiner, Professor of New Testament Interpretation, The Southern Baptist Theological Seminary
Dr. Moises Silva, B.A., Bob Jones University, BD, Westminster Theological Seminary, ThM, Westminster Theological Seminary, Ph.D., University of Manchester *(Naturally, Moises, having graduated from BJU would have been trained to believe the Critical text was superior to the Textus Receptus. Therefore it is no surprise he "served as a translator of the New American Standard Bible, the New Living Translation (Ephesians - Philemon), the English Standard Version and the Nueva Versión Internacional, and as a New Testament consultant for Eugene Peterson's The Message."*[58]*)*
Dr. Frank S. Thielman, Associate Professor of Divinity, Beeson Divinity School
Dr. Willem A. VanGemeren, Professor of Old Testament and Semitic Studies, Director of the PhD in Theological Studies, Trinity Evangelical Divinity School
Dr. James W. Voelz, Professor of Exegetical Theology, Concordia Seminary, St. Louis, Mo.
Dr. Daniel B. Wallace, Professor of New Testament Studies, Dallas Theological Seminary *(Daniel B. Wallace is the well-known professor at Dallas Seminary who travels the world to study Greek manuscripts. Wallace is also known for his antagonism for the King James Bible and its Greek text. He says "the King James Bible is filled with readings which have been created by overly zealous scribes! Very few of the distinctive King James readings are demonstrably ancient".*[59] *Wallace is correct when he says "Westcott and Hort were able to convince the vast majority of New Testament scholars of the truth*

---

[58] http://en.wikipedia.org/wiki/Mois%C3%A9s_Silva

[59] https://bible.org/article/why-i-do-not-think-king-james-bible-best-tranlation-available-tod

of their textual choices. Essentially, they argued that the Greek text behind the KJV NT was inferior and late."⁶⁰ Wallace is truthful when he writes that W & H "preferred the five great uncial MSS (known by their letters, Aleph, A, B, C, D), all of which dated from the fourth or fifth century, as well as early versional and patristic evidence. Two MSS in particular, B and Aleph, were favorites of WH. Both came from the fourth century." Most if not all of these men in this group would agree with W & H on this.)

    Dr. Dean O. Wenthe, President, Concordia Theological Seminary, Fort Wayne, IN

    Dr. Walter W. Wessel, Former Professor of New Testament, Bethel Seminary—West

    Dr. Robert W. Yarbrough, Associate Professor of New Testament, Trinity Evangelical Divinity School

    DID YOU FIND ONE MAN THAT YOU WOULD CLASSIFY AS A FUNDAMENTALIST? Yes, there are some conservatives within this group but "ULTRA-CONSERVATIVE"?

Some of the people who are endorsing the ESV are Francis Chan, John Piper, Darrin Patrick (The Journey Church), David Platt, Tullian Tchividjian (Coral Ridge Presbyterian Church), Thabiti Anyabwile, Mark D. Roberts, Mary Kassian, Paul McCain (Luthern), Janet Parshall, Matt Chandler, recording artist Lecrae, Kevin DeYoung and Elyse Fitxpatrick.⁶¹ Then there is Mark Driscoll who says: *"The ESV Study Bible is the most important resource that has been given to the **emerging** generation of Bible students and teachers. The ESV Study Bible is the best. Period."*⁶²

It is due to this popularity among such well known voices and the wild abandonment of the King James Bible that this review is being written.

Now, before getting into the review, it is interesting to read what a rising star within the GARBC has to say about folk such as we who comprise the Dean

---

⁶⁰ https://bible.org/article/conspiracy-behind-new-bible-translations

⁶¹ http://www.esv.org/esv/endorsements/trusted-by-leaders/

⁶² http://www.esv.org/esvsb/endorsements/

Burgon Society. Dr Kevin Bauder (Research Professor of Systematic Theology, Central Seminary, Plymouth, MN.) says there are:
> "*eight characteristics of hyper-fundamentalism,*" a group he calls "*the noisiest and often the most visible representatives of fundamentalism.*"[63]

One of the noisy eight Dr Bauder mentions is those who take a:
> "*Militant stance regarding some extra-biblical or even anti-biblical teaching, such as commitment to a theory of textual preservation and Biblical translation that leaves the King James Version as the only acceptable English Bible.*"[64]

I am sure we in the DBS would fit into this category! Of course Dr Bauder is one of those who continues to use the King James in his teaching and preaching but corrects it whenever he feels it and its underlying Greek text are wrong.

Now to the review of the ESV. The following is taken directly from the ESV web site. The bold type has been added by this writer and my remarks are in brackets and italics.

---

[63] http://baptistbulletin.org/?p=19073

[64] *Ibid.*

About the ESV Translation[65]
Translation Philosophy

"The ESV is an 'essentially literal' translation that seeks as far as possible to capture the precise wording of the original text and the personal style of each Bible writer. As such, its emphasis is on 'word-for-word' correspondence, at the same time taking into account differences of grammar, syntax, and idiom between current literary English and the original languages. Thus it seeks to be transparent to the original text, letting the reader see as directly as possible the structure and meaning of the original.

In contrast to the ESV, some Bible versions have followed a 'thought-for-thought' rather than 'word-for-word' translation philosophy, emphasizing 'dynamic equivalence' rather than the 'essentially literal' meaning of the original. A 'thought-for-thought' translation is of necessity more inclined to reflect the interpretive opinions of the translator and the influences of contemporary culture.

Every translation is at many points a trade-off between literal precision and readability, between 'formal equivalence' in expression and 'functional equivalence' in communication, and the ESV is no exception. Within this framework we have sought to be 'as literal as possible' while maintaining clarity of expression and literary excellence.

Therefore, to the extent that plain English permits and the meaning in each case allows, we have sought to use the same English word for important recurring words in the original; and, as far as grammar and syntax allow, we have rendered Old Testament passages cited in the New in ways that show their correspondence. Thus in each of these areas, as well as

---

[65] http://www.esv.org/esv/translation/about/

throughout the Bible as a whole, we have sought to capture the echoes and overtones of meaning that are so abundantly present in the original texts.

As an essentially literal translation, then, the ESV seeks to carry over every possible nuance of meaning in the original words of Scripture into our own language. As such, it is ideally suited for in-depth study of the Bible. Indeed, with its emphasis on literary excellence, the ESV is equally suited for public reading and preaching, for private reading and reflection, for both academic and devotional study, and for Scripture memorization.

Manuscripts Used in Translating the ESV

Each word and phrase in the ESV has been carefully weighed against *the original Hebrew, Aramaic, and Greek*, to ensure the fullest accuracy and clarity and to avoid under-translating or overlooking any nuance of the original text. *(As one reads on you might wonder where the ESV translators considered the original Hebrew, Aramaic, and Greek words and texts to be found?) (It depends on what one considers to be the original Hebrew, Aramaic, and Greek texts? Not surprisingly the ESV translators considered texts not underlying the King James Bible as the original texts.)*

The words and phrases themselves grow out of the Tyndale-King James legacy, and most recently out of the RSV, with the 1971 RSV text providing the starting point for our work. [If they follow the Tyndale-King James legacy then they cannot follow the 1971 RSV text for the two are different! Remember, if they are different they are not the same! DB]

Archaic language has been brought to current usage and **significant corrections** have been made in the translation of **key texts**. But throughout, our goal has been to retain the depth of meaning and enduring language that have made their indelible mark on the English-speaking world and have defined the life and doctrine of the church over the last four centuries.

The ESV is based on the Masoretic text of the Hebrew Bible as found in Biblia Hebraica Stuttgartensia (2nd ed., 1983), and on the Greek text in the 1993 editions of the Greek New Testament (4th corrected ed.), published by the United Bible Societies (UBS), and Novum Testamentum Graece (27th ed.), edited by Nestle and Aland. [Dr Kirk DiVietro did an excellent job of explaining these Hebrew texts at the

2013 DBS meeting. The ESV cannot follow the King James legacy if it is based on a different Greek text as it admits it is. If they are different they are NOT THE SAME! DB]

The currently renewed respect among Old Testament scholars for the Masoretic text is reflected in the ESV's attempt, wherever possible, to translate difficult Hebrew passages as they stand in the Masoretic text rather than resorting to emendations or to finding an alternative reading in the ancient versions.

In exceptional, difficult cases, the Dead Sea Scrolls, the Septuagint, the Samaritan Pentateuch, the Syriac Peshitta, the Latin Vulgate, and other sources were consulted** to shed possible light on the text, or, if necessary, to support a divergence from the Masoretic text.* ***Similarly, in a few difficult cases in the New Testament, the ESV has followed a Greek text different from the text given preference in the UBS/Nestle-Aland 27th edition. [Dr Kirk DiVietro did a superb job in his presentation in 2013 when he dealt with the Masoretic text of the Hebrew Bible underlying the King James Bible and the *Biblia Hebraica Stuttgartensia* underlying the ESV and other new versions. It seems those translating the new versions so often just pick and choose. Some of the other sources these new versions pick and choose folk use are; the Dead Sea Scrolls, the Septuagint, the Samaritan Pentateuch, the Syriac Peshitta and the Latin Vulgate. Dr DiVietro's paper is worth reading. DB]

The footnotes that accompany the ESV text inform the reader of textual variations and difficulties and show how these have been resolved by the ESV Translation Team. In addition to this, the footnotes indicate significant alternative readings and occasionally provide an explanation for technical terms or for a difficult reading in the text. [These footnotes are not faith-building in the life of a believer. They would certainly not give one confidence in the Bible they read. DB]

Dean John Burgon's Defense of the Authorized Version   75

Throughout, the Translation Team has benefited greatly from the massive textual resources that have become readily available recently, from new insights into biblical laws and culture, and from current advances in Hebrew and Greek lexicography and grammatical understanding. [What massive textual resources have become readily available? As Dr DiVietro said in 2013 (I am paraphrasing) when they made changes to the Old Testament it wasn't because of the Hebrew text but due to the translators just making a change for changes sake. DB]

Since the ESV was originally published in 2001 it has gone through two revisions. The first was in 2007 and the latest is 2011. However, the publisher assures the reader the changes are very few when they say; "The extent of the word changes is comparatively small, involving about 275 verses and less than 500 words out of more than 750,000 words in the Bible text. To put this into perspective, the changes to the ESV are about one one-hundredth of the changes made recently in other leading Bible translations."

A few examples are changes from 'yourself' to 'you'; from 'servant' to 'worker'; from 'has not' to 'does not have'; from 'young man' to 'boy'; from 'capital' to 'citadel'; from 'bondage' to 'slavery'; from 'nor' to 'or'; from 'trustworthy' to faithful'; from 'competent' to 'sufficient'; from 'everyone' to 'each one.'"[66]

Since the 2011 ESV is the latest version it is that version that will be used in this review. In this review, there will be comparisons of the ESV 2011 text, along with the text of the King James New Testament as found in the "Doctored" New Testament.[67] The changes Westcott and Hort (W&H) made in their New Greek Text, and which the ESV often follows, will be in brackets after the KJB reading. It should be understood that if W&H and those following

---

* http://bible-researcher.com/esv2011changes.pdf p. 1

' D. A. Waite, Jr., *The "Doctored" new Testament*, The Bible For Today Press, 900 Park venue, Collingswood, NJ 08108.

their lead, only make one change and get by with that change, that means they have been given the liberty to make other changes later. The ESV's copyright allows us to quote 500 verses but we will fall short of that for this review.

A good resource book that covers **all the changes** WH did to the Greek and English texts can be found in Dr Jack Moorman's *8,000 Differences*.[68] Dr Waite writes in the Foreword of Dr Moorman's book that the book is vindicated when even fundamentalist leaders teach

> "that there are very few differences between the New Testament Greek texts of Westcott and Hort, Nestle/Aland, or United Bible Societies and the Greek Words underlying our King James Bible. Here is a tabulation of **over 8,000 differences between these two kinds of Greek New Testament texts**. The differences are in the Greek Words, but the English translations are also given to show where the changes affect translation. Some of the differences do not affect the English translation, but they are differences nonetheless. **There are over 356 of these differences that affect Bible doctrines in one way or another** (Emphasis added)."[69]

Here are a few of the differences between the ESV and the King James Bible.

ESV Mark 16:19-20 is bracketed. (*"In their margin, WH indicated that verses 9-20 are missing in certain ancient authorities and that some have a different ending to Mark's Gospel."* What is amazing is that the translators of these new versions agree with WH but they continue to put the verses in their translation howbeit with brackets and notes. John Burgon in his Defense of these verse says "Professor Westcott--who, jointly with the Rev. F. J. A. Hort, announces a revised Text--assures us that 'the original text, from whatever cause it may have happened, terminated abruptly after the account of the Angelic vision.' The rest 'was added at another time, and probably by another hand.'" Bracketing Mark 16:19-20 is typical of those following W & H. Are these verses

---

[68] J. A. Moorman, *8,000 Differences*, The Bible For Today, 900 Park Ave., Collingswood, 08108

[69] J. A. Moorman, *8,000 Differences*, The Bible For Today, 900 Park Ave., Collingswood, 08108, p. iii.

Dean John Burgon's Defense of the Authorized Version 77

true or spurious? If false, leave them out but if true print them without the brackets and unbelieving footnotes!)

ESV John 7:53-8:11 is bracketed. *("In their text, WH put John 7:53-John 8:11 in brackets. In their margin, WH virtually rejected the passage."* Dean John William Burgon in The Revision Revised writes on page 309 that Hort *"is of opinion that the Woman taken in Adultery (filling 12 verses), 'presents serious differences from the diction of S. John's Gospel,'—treats it as 'an insertion in a comparatively late Western text' and declines to retain it even within brackets, on the ground that it 'would fatally interrupt' the course of the narrative if suffered to stand'. On pages 311, 312 John Burgon wrote in a footnote "in vii. 53 to viii. 11, the narrative concerning the woman taken in adultery omitted,—concerning which Drs. W. and H. remark that 'the argument which has always told most in its favour in modern times is its own internal character. The story itself has justly seemed to vouch for its own substantial truth, and the words in which it is clothed to harmonize with those of other Gospel narratives'").*

ESV Acts 1:8: *"But you will receive power when the Holy Spirit has come upon you, and you will be <u>my witnesses</u> in Jerusalem and in all Judea and Samaria, and to the end of the earth."*

Ac 1:8: *"But ye shall receive power, after that the Holy Ghost is come upon you: and ye shall be witnesses <u>unto me</u> both in Jerusalem, and in all Judaea, and in Samaria, and unto the uttermost part of the earth."* (KJV) *("WH changed <u>unto me</u> (moi) to of me (mou).* **Dative** *Singular to* **Genitive** *Singular [case] ." That change may not seem like much of a difference to those of us who are not proficient in the original language but it is a change and it does make a difference when translating. If they can make one change they can make many, many more changes, which they do!)*

ESV Acts 1:10: *"And while they were gazing into heaven as he went, behold, two men stood by them in <u>white robes</u>."*

Ac 1:10: *"And while they looked stedfastly toward heaven as he went up, behold, two men stood by them in <u>white apparel</u>;* (KJV) **("***WH changed <u>white apparel (esthAti leukA)</u> to white apparels (<u>esthAsesi leukais</u>) Dative Feminine*

Singular *to Dative Feminine* **Plural** *[number]" Small change BUT it is a change!)*

ESV Acts 1:11: *"and said, Men of Galilee, why do you stand <u>looking</u> into heaven? This Jesus, who was taken up from you into heaven, will come in the same way as you saw him go into heaven."*

Acts 1:11: *"Which also said, Ye men of Galilee, why stand ye <u>gazing up</u> into heaven? this same Jesus, which is taken up from you into heaven, shall so come in like manner as ye have seen him go into heaven."* (KJV) *("WH changed gazing up (**em**blepontes) to gazing (blepontes). [prefix dropped]" Instead of "gazing" the ESV has "looking.")*

ESV Acts 1:13: *"And when they had entered, <u>they went up to the upper room</u>, where they were staying, Peter and <u>John</u> and <u>James</u> and Andrew, Philip and Thomas, Bartholomew and Matthew, James the son of Alphaeus and Simon the Zealot and Judas the son of James."*

Acts 1:13: *"And when they were come in, <u>they went up into an upper room</u>, where abode both Peter, and James, and John, and Andrew, Philip, and Thomas, Bartholomew, and Matthew, James the son of Alphaeus, and Simon Zelotes, and Judas the brother of James."* (KJV) *("WH changed the word order from <u>THEY WENT UP</u> into the upper room to into the upper room THEY WENT UP. WH changed the word order from <u>James</u> and <u>John</u> to <u>John</u> and <u>James</u>." Why do you think they made these small changes? Could it be that if you can get by making small changes without question you can then make bigger changes?)*

ESV Acts 1:14: *"All these with one accord were devoting themselves to prayer, together with the women and Mary the mother of Jesus, and his brothers."* (The ESV has the following footnote *"Or brothers and sisters. The plural Greek word adelphoi (translated "brothers") refers to siblings in a family. In New Testament usage, depending on the context, adelphoi may refer either to men or to both men and women who are siblings (brothers and sisters) in God's family, the church; also verse 15."* What do you believe is the underlying purpose of this footnote?)

Acts 1:14: "*These all continued with one accord in prayer <u>and supplication</u>, with the women, and Mary the mother of Jesus, and with his brethren.*" (KJV) *("WH omitted and the supplication (kai tA deAse)" The ESV follows suit in omitting the words. Why would the "intolerable" texts of WH leave out supplication? Are those following the ESV losing something important? Even though the two, prayer and supplication, are similar they are different words. To pray includes requesting but supplication is more intense and includes an urging of the petition for which we have prayed.)*

ESV Acts 1:15: "*In those days Peter stood up among the <u>brothers</u> (the company of persons was in all about 120) and said*"

Acts 1:15: "*And in those days Peter stood up in the midst of the <u>disciples</u>, and said, (the number of names together were about an hundred and twenty,)*" (KJV) *("WH changed <u>disciples</u> (<u>mathAtOn</u>) to brethren (adelfOn)" Why would the texts that WH followed change the word from disciples to brethren? A disciple is a follower, a learner of the Lord Jesus. Yes, they were brethren through faith in the Lord Jesus Christ but they were more than brethren, they were disciples, followers of the Lord Jesus Christ.)*

ESV Acts 2:30: "*Being therefore a prophet, and knowing that God had sworn with an oath to him that he would set one of his descendants on his throne*"

Acts 2:30: "*Therefore being a prophet, and knowing that God had sworn with an oath to him, that of the fruit of his loins, <u>according to the flesh, he would raise up Christ</u> to sit on his throne;*" (KJV) *("WH omitted the according to the flesh to raise up the Christ (to kata sarka anastAsein ton criston)" These omitted words strengthen the Lord's humanity, right to David's throne and His resurrection.)*

ESV Acts 8:36: "*And as they were going along the road they came to some water, and the eunuch said, 'See, here is water! What prevents me from being baptized?'*" *(The ESV has this footnote "Some manuscripts add all or most of verse 37: And Philip said, "If you believe with all your heart, you may." And he replied, "I believe that Jesus Christ is the Son of God."*
How does this build confidence in the Word of God?)*

Acts 8:36: "*And as they went on their way, they came unto a certain water: and the eunuch said, See, here is water; what doth hinder me to be baptized? 37 And Philip said, If thou believest with all thine heart, thou mayest. And he answered and said, I believe that Jesus Christ is the Son of God.*" (KJV) *("WH omitted all of Acts 8:37. This verse is an open declaration of one's confession of faith in the deity of the Lord Jesus Christ as their personal Saviour.)*

ESV Acts 9:6: "*But rise and enter the city, and you will be told what you are to do.*"

Acts 9:6: "*And he trembling and astonished said, Lord, what wilt thou have me to do? And the Lord said unto him, Arise, and go into the city, and it shall be told thee what thou must do.*" (KJV) *("WH omitted <u>and he trembling and astonished said Lord what wilt thou have me to do? and the Lord said unto him</u>" Paul's reaction was typical of a mere human who was in the presence of God and his submission to the will of the Lord for his life.)*

ESV Acts 15:24: "*Since we have heard that some persons have gone out from us and troubled you with words, unsettling your minds, although we gave them no instructions,*"

Acts 15:24: "*Forasmuch as we have heard, that certain which went out from us have troubled you with words, subverting your souls, <u>saying, Ye must be circumcised, and keep the law: to whom we gave no such commandment</u>:*" *("WH omitted <u>saying, Ye must be circumcised, and keep the law: to whom we gave no such commandment</u>." These men were teaching wrong doctrine!)*

ESV Romans 14:23: "*But whoever has doubts is condemned if he eats, because the eating is not from faith. For whatever does not proceed from faith is sin.*" *(The ESV has the footnote "Some manuscripts insert here 16:25-27" The ESV continue to put doubts in the mind of the reader as to the reliability of the Word of God.)*

ESV Galatians 5:19: "*Now the works of the flesh are evident: sexual immorality, impurity, sensuality,*"

Galatians 5:19: "*Now the works of the flesh are manifest, which are these; Adultery, fornication, uncleanness, lasciviousness,*" (KJV) *("WH omitted adultery (moiceia).*" Spurgeon said of this verse *"No matter what they profess, or what sacraments they may partake of, those who live in these sins are not alive unto God. What a list we have here! Surely sin is a prolific mother.*" Do you think the modern translators may enjoy omitting the sin of adultery due to present sin or some skeletons in the closet? Of course the commentaries such as Jamison-Fausset-Brown follow the leading of W&H when they tell the reader *"Adultery--omitted in the oldest manuscripts."*)

Enough has been shown to see that the ever popular ESV is just another version following the W&H line. The same old song is sung concerning the poor old King James Bible and that is:

> "*The KJV was a great literal translation in its day, but that day was the 17th century! Many earlier and more accurate biblical manuscripts were discovered afterwards and most modern translations—including those produced by very conservative Christians—are based on them.*"[70]

The above writer even says the manuscripts upon which the King James is based are the "*less accurate manuscripts*" because they were not "*available to the KJV translators in the 17th century.*"[71] Does all that sound too familiar?

However, Dean John William Burgon quotes Scrivener when he wrote:

> "*It is no less true to fact than paradoxical in sound, that the worst corruptions to which the New Testament has ever been subjected, originated within a hundred years after it was composed; that Irenaeus and the African Fathers and the whole Western, with a portion of the Syriac Church, used far inferior manuscripts to those employed by Stunica, or Erasmus, or Stephen, thirteen centuries after, when moulding the Textus Receptus.*"[72]

[ ] http://courses.missouristate.edu/markgiven/rel102/bt.htm

[1] *Ibid.*

[2] Dean John William Burgon, THE TRADITIONAL TEXT OF THE HOLY GOSPELS, Vol. 1, Dean Burgon Society Press, Box 354, Collingswood, NJ 08108, p. 40.

John Burgon agreed saying that

> "*No sooner was the work of Evangelists and Apostles recognized as the necessary counterpart and complement of God's ancient Scriptures and became the 'New Testament,' than a reception was found to be awaiting it in the world closely resembling that which He experienced Who is the subject of its pages. Calumny and misrepresentation, persecution and murderous hate, assailed Him continually. And the Written Word in like manner, in the earliest age of all, was shamefully handled by mankind. Not only was it confused through human infirmity and misapprehension, but it became also the object of restless malice and unsparing assaults. Marcion, Valentinus, Basilides, Heracleon, Menander, Asclepiades, Theodotus, Hermophilus, Apollonides, and other heretics, adapted the Gospels to their own ideas. Tatian, and later on Ammonius, created confusion through attempts to combine the four Gospels either in a diatessaron or upon an intricate arrangement made by sections, under which as a further result the words of one Gospel became assimilated to those of another. Want of familiarity with the sacred words in the first ages, carelessness of scribes, incompetent teaching, and ignorance of Greek in the West, led to further corruption of the Sacred Text. Then out of the fact that there existed a vast number of corrupt copies arose at once the need of Recension, which was carried on by Origen and his [Gnostic] school. This was a fatal necessity to have made itself felt in an age when the first principles of the Science were not understood; for 'to correct' was too often in those days another word for 'to corrupt.' And this is the first thing to be briefly explained and enforced: but more than a counterbalance was provided under the overruling Providence of God.*"[73]

As the Dean states he was:

> ". . . *utterly disinclined to believe—so grossly improbable does it seem—that at the end of 1800 years 995 copies out*

---

[73] *Ibid.*, pp. 10, 11.

of every thousand, suppose, will prove untrustworthy; and that the one, two, three, four or five which remain, whose contents were till yesterday as good as unknown, will be found to have retained the secret of what the Holy Spirit originally inspired. I am utterly unable to believe, in short, that God's promise has so entirely failed, that at the end of 1800 years much of the text of the Gospel had in point of fact to be picked by a German critic out of a waste-paper basket in the convent of St. Catherine; and that the entire text had to be remodelled after the pattern set by a couple of copies which had remained in neglect during fifteen centuries, and had probably owed their survival to that neglect; whilst hundreds of others had been thumbed to pieces, and had bequeathed their witness to copies made from them."[74]

Yes, it is true that:

"In short, the Traditional Text, founded upon the vast majority of authorities and upon the Rock of Christ's Church, will, if I mistake not, be found upon examination to be out of all comparison superior to a text of the nineteenth century, whatever skill and ingenuity may have been expended upon the production or the Defense of it."[75]

From the first century to the nineteenth, most of Christendom believed those texts that came to be known as the Textus Receptus were the Words of God. The churches were content and happy to use them as they believed they were faithful to those Words that God had originally breathed out. Therefore those manuscripts of the fourth century were rejected and spurned by the churches. The churches knew the history of the Received Traditional Text for this Text has a pedigree which:

"goes step by step in unbroken succession regularly back to the earliest time. The present printed editions may be compared for extreme accuracy with the text passed by the

---

[4] Ibid., p. 12.

[5] Dean John William Burgon, THE TRADITIONAL TEXT OF THE HOLY GOSPELS, Vol. 1, Dean Burgon Society Press, Box 354, Collingswood, NJ 08108, p. 13.

> Elzevirs or Beza as the text received by all of their time. Erasmus followed his few MSS. because he knew them to be good representatives of the mind of the Church which had been informed under the ceaseless and loving care of mediaeval transcribers . . ."[76]

Yes, we can be assured we have the inspired Words of God which underlie our King James Bible and are faithfully and accurately translated over into the King James Bible. The ESV is not of that heritage in spite of the ESV promoters saying *"the legacy established first in the Tyndale New Testament (1526) and the KJV Bible (1611)"*[77] is that of the ESV! The ESV's heritage is based on W&H's:

> *"finespun theories and technical terms, such as 'Intrinsic Probability,' 'Transcriptional Probability,' 'Internal evidence of Readings,' 'Internal evidence of Documents,' which, of course, connote a certain amount of evidence, but are weak pillars of a heavy structure."*[78]

I agree with Dean John William Burgon when he wrote that

> *". . . we bow to the teaching of the HOLY GHOST, as conveyed in all wisdom by facts and evidence: and we are certain, that, following no preconceived notions of our own, but led under such guidance, moved by principles so reasonable and comprehensive, and observing rules and instructions appealing to us with such authority, we are in all main respects STANDING UPON THE ROCK."*[79]

---

[76] *Ibid.*, p. 236.

[77] http://www.esv.org/esv/history/legacy/

[78] *Ibid.*, p.238.

[79] *Ibid.*, p. 239

Index of Words, Phrases, and Scriptures

100-member team 65
1008AD 49
14% 39
1598 .... 13, 48
1831 .... 46, 47
1870 .... 11, 18, 30
1881 .... 9, 13, 15, 16, 26, 27, 29, 33-35
1881 English Revised Version 9
190 places 13
190 places from other sources 13
1906 and 1912 48
1932 .... 37, 42
1937 48
1948-53 48
1952 RSV 51
1961 41-45
1971 .... 9, 49-51, 73
1971 RSV 9, 49, 51, 73
1971 RSV text 9, 73
1993 editions of the Greek 9, 47, 73
1994 .... iii, 39
2 Peter 1:5-7 23
2001 .... 39, 40, 51, 65, 75
2005 39
2007 75
2011 .... iv, 43, 45, 58, 61, 75
275 verses 75
2nd Rabbinic Bible 48
32 thousand quotes from the New Testament 54
325 .... 53, 54
350-plus copies 53
356 76
36,000 changes 30
382 to 405 53
400 years 48

500 more COPIES 19
500 words 75
6000 times 17
750,000 words 75
8,000 Differences 4, 76
90 millions of English-speaking Christians 26
995 copies out of every thousand 83
A. V. 22, 24, 25
ABANDONMENT OF THE KING JAMES BIBLE 37, 40, 69
aberrant theology 57
About the ESV Translation .... iv, 71
ABWE .... iii, 39, 66
accuracy 6, 50, 52, 54, 73, 83
Acts 18:7 13
African Fathers 81
AGENCIES LEAVEN THE CHURCHES 58
Aland 3, 9, 48, 73, 74, 76
Allah 38
Allen Wikgren 3
American Standard Version 3, 41, 43, 61
American Standard Version of 1901 3
Ammonius 82
Amplified Bible 43, 61, 62
Amplified New Testament 43
ancient Lectionaries 19
ancient versions 19, 74
Ankeny, IA 3
annual conference .... ii, 59
ante Nicene fathers 54
Antiquity 7
Aorist 23
Apollonides 82
apostate 3, 49
APPENDIX 1 .... iv, 3, 37, 61
APPENDIX 2 .... iv, 22, 61
approval system 37, 56, 57
Archaic language 73
Asclepiades 82
August 21, 1813--August 4, 1888 4

Dean John Burgon's Defense of the Authorized Version 87

Authorized Bible 26
Authorized Version .... I, iii, iv, I, 3, 7-21, 23-35, 39
AV John 17:4 22
aversion 34
Awana 58
Baloche 58
Baptist ...... i-iv, 3-5, 29, 31, 35-37, 39, 41-43, 45, 47, 56-59, 61, 62, 66-68, 70
Baptist Bible College and Seminary 47
Baptist Bulletin 41-43, 45, 62
Baptist college 3, 58, 59, 67
Baptist colleges 3
BAPTIST FELLOWSHIPS .... iv, 37, 56
Baptist in its name 58
Baptist schools 35, 36
Baptists in America 35
Basilides 82
Bauder 70
Ben Asher Masoretic Text 48
Ben Chayyim in 1524-25 48
Bennett .... I, iii, I-3, 59
Bethany Theological Seminary 4
better manuscripts 46
Beza 13, 50, 84
Beza's N. T. of 1598 13
Bible For Today Baptist Church .... i-iii, 39
Bible versions 39, 41, 43, 71
Biblia Hebraica 47-49, 73, 74
Biblia Hebraica Stuttgartensia 47, 73, 74
Bishop Ellicott 17, 28
Bishop Wordsworth 30
Black 3
Bob Jones University 47, 68
Bodmer Papyri 50, 53
Bomberg 48
Brenton Brown 58
Broughton 34
Brown 58, 81
Bruce M. Metzger 3
Burgon .... iii, 1-31, 33-36, 42, 46, 47, 59, 70, 76, 77, 81-84

Butrin 41-45
By The Word 20, 23, 38
Bynum 5
Calvary Baptist Theological Seminary 47
Cambridge University Press 29
Cardinal 3
Carlo M. Martini 3
CCM 58, 59
CCM IS NOT THE PROBLEM 59
Cedarville 58
Cedarville University 58
Central Baptist Theological Seminary 47
Central Seminary 5, 70
Chairman of the New Testament Company 28
changes 7, 10-13, 21-23, 27, 30, 31, 50, 75-78
Charles T. Butrin 41
Chris Tomlin 58
Christendom 6, 33, 83
church fathers 54
Church of England 30, 32, 33
Cicero 3
codex B 14, 50, 53
Codex Bezae 50
collated 19
Community Fellowship 58
Consent of Witnesses 7
conservatives 2, 12, 36, 57, 63, 69
Constantine 53
Continuity 7
convent of St. Catherine 83
Convocation 11, 18, 20, 30, 31
Convocation of the Southern Province 11, 18
copyright .... i, 49, 51, 76
Coral Ridge Presbyterian Church 69
Corban University 59
Cornerstone University 58
correction 6, 36
Council of 18 57
Council of Eighteen 43, 58, 61, 62

Council of Nicea 53, 54
Critical Greek Text .... I, 2, 35, 36, 44, 46, 51, 55, 61
Critical Text 16, 19, 35, 46, 59, 62, 68
D A Waite 5
D O Fuller 5
D. A. Waite, Jr 75
Dallas 3, 5, 48, 49, 66-68
Dallas Seminary 3, 5, 68
Daniel B. Wallace 5, 68
Daniel Bomberg 48
David C. Bennett .... I, I, 3, 59
DBS iii-5, 7, 8, 23, 28, 59, 70, 74
Dead Sea Scrolls 74
Dean Burgon .... iii, 1-7, 36, 59, 70, 81, 83
Dean Burgon Society .... iii, 2-7, 36, 59, 70, 81, 83
Dean John Burgon .... I, 7
Dean John William Burgon .... I, 6, 7, 36, 46, 77, 81, 83, 84
Dean of Chichester .... I, 4
deceivers 11
DEFENDING THE KING JAMES BIBLE 4, 48, 49
deprecate 8, 18
deprecate it entirely 8, 18
dethrone the Greek Text 29
Detroit Baptist Theological Seminary 39, 47
diligently collated 19
distrust 34
DiVietro 73-75
Division of Christian Education 51
doctrines 76
Dothan, Alabama 4
Dr Bauder 70
Dr DiVietro 75
Dr Kevin Bauder 70
Dr Robert T. Ketcham 42
Dr Thomas Strouse 44
Dr Viggo Olsen 38
Dr Waite 76
Dr. D. A. Waite 7, 37, 48
Dr. Daniel B. Wallace 68

Dr. G. Vance Smith 31
Dr. Hort 26
Dr. Lachmann 46
Dr. Merrill F. Unger 48
Dr. Moises Silva 68
Dr. Scrivener 29
Dr. Vance Smith 33
Dr. Waite 48, 49
Dress standards seem to go down 40
dress, songs, and worship 56
Driscoll 69
Drs. Westcott and Hort 15, 19
dynamic equivalency 38
E L Bynum 5
earlier texts 55
early church fathers 54
Eastern Orthodox 51
Ecumenical 51
Edward Miller 5
Egypt 59
eight thousand ancient copies 53
eight thousand places 4
Elizabethan English 45
Ellicott 17, 28, 30
Elzevirs 84
English Reader 25
English Revised Version .... iii, 2, 4, 9, 16, 36
ENGLISH STANDARD VERSION 2011 .... iv, 61
Erasmus 6, 81, 84
ERRORS 30, 31, 34
essentially literal 72
essentially literal translation 72
ESV .... iv, 9, 16, 22, 35, 39, 40, 46-49, 51, 52, 55, 61-63, 65, 69-81, 84
ESV Acts 1:10 77
ESV Acts 1:11 78
ESV Acts 1:13 78
ESV Acts 1:14 78
ESV Acts 1:15 79
ESV Acts 1:8 77

ESV Acts 15:24	80
ESV Acts 2:30	79
ESV Acts 8:36	79
ESV Acts 9:6	80
ESV Galatians 5:19	80
ESV John 17:4	22
ESV John 7:53-8:11	77
ESV Mark 16:19-20	76
ESV Romans 14:23	80
ESV Translation Team	74
Eugene Nida	38
Eusebius	54, 55
Evidence of the Entire Passage	7
external evidence	55
Faith Baptist Bible College	3, 41, 47
Faith Baptist Bible College and Seminary	47
faithful and trustworthy King James Bible	28
faithfully and helpfully	34
false Hebrew texts	49
fatal error	12
FATHERS	19, 26, 54, 81
FBBC	3, 4
Feb. 10th, 1870	11, 30
FEW AS POSSIBLE	20
field council meetings	39
fifty years (1831-81)	47
Fuller	5, 24
fundamental	10, 11, 19, 47
fundamentalist	45, 59, 65, 66, 69, 76
fundamentalist brethren	59
GARB	37-47, 51, 56-59, 61, 62, 69
GARB mission board	37
GARBC Council of Eighteen	43, 62
GARBC National Representative	42
Gary Hudson	59
General Association of Regular Baptist Churches	37, 61
Genesis 2:18	37
German	3, 11, 12, 42, 44-47, 56, 83
German critic	83

German prejudices 11, 12, 46
German rationalism 45, 46
German school of Textual Criticism 46
Gertrude Grace Sanborn 36
giants 21
Gnostic 1, 2
God blessed for ever 26
Godhead 32
Grand Rapids Baptist Seminary 4
Grand Rapids School of Bible 41
Grassi 39, 40, 51
GRBS 4
Greek scholars 23
Greek Text 1-5, 9, 11-13, 15-20, 29-32, 35-37, 41, 42, 44-47, 51, 55, 56, 58,
59, 61, 68-70, 73-75
grievous lack of Taste 25
grossly depraved NEW GREEK TEXT 17
harmonizer 16
Hebrew, Aramaic, and Greek Words ii-5, 44, 73
Heracleon 82
heretics 82
Hermophilus 82
historian 3
historic position 57
historic position of the GARBC 57
history 3, 34, 52, 56, 83, 84
Holman Christian Standard Bible 43, 61, 62
Hudson 59
Hugh Broughton 34
Hughes 58
incompetent men 20
independent Baptist colleges 3
infection 57, 58
inspired 6, 14, 19, 20, 36, 44, 83, 84
inspired Original 19, 44
Internal Considerations 7
Irenaeus 54, 81
James Richard May 4
Jeff Straub 5, 45

Jerome 54
Jerusalem Chamber 10, 14, 21, 34
Joel R. Grassi 39, 40, 51
John 14:6 3
John 17:17 3
John 17:4 & 6 21
John 17:6 22
John 7.53-8.11 50
John Burgon 1, 5, 7-31, 33-35, 46, 47, 76, 77, 82
John MacArthur 51, 55, 56
John Piper 69
John William Burgon 1, 4-8, 36, 42, 46, 47, 77, 81, 83, 84
Justin Martyr 54
Ketcham 42, 43
King James Bible .. i-iv, 1, 3-6, 9, 11, 13, 28, 36, 37, 39-42, 44-46, 48, 49, 55, 56, 58, 59, 61, 62, 68, 69, 73, 74, 76, 81, 84
King James Only 3
Kittel 48, 49
Kurt Aland 3
Lachmann 46
later texts 55
Latin 15, 16, 49, 53, 54, 74
Latin Vulgate 54, 74
Lectionaries 19
left the GARBC-approved mission agency 39
legendum 49
Leningrad Codex 48
Leningrad Manuscript, (B19a or 'L' 49
liberal theology 43, 44
liberal translation 43
liberals 36
literal 41, 65, 71, 72, 81
literal translation 41, 72, 81
Litmus Test for Orthodoxy 45
Los Angeles Baptist Seminary 57
Luke 22.19b-20 50
Luke 22.43-44 50
Luke 24:10 16
Lynn Silvernale 38

MacArthur 51, 55, 56
Manuscripts Used in Translating the ESV .... iv, 73
Many denominations 65
Marcion 82
Mark 14, 25, 26, 50, 52, 53, 69, 73, 76
Mark 11:8 14
Mark 16.9-20 50
Mark Driscoll 69
Martini 3
Masoretic Hebrew text 48
Masoretic text 44, 47-49, 73, 74
Master's Seminary 55, 56, 66
Matt Redman 58
Matthew 3, 21, 25, 26, 38, 78
Matthew Black 3
medieval text 55
Menander 82
methodological infection 57, 58
Metzger 3
Miller 5, 62
mission .... ii, iii, 37-39, 46, 80
mission board 37
Moorman 4, 76
Muhammad 38
music 8, 41, 56, 58
Muslim 38
My Treasure, my Comfort 36
Myths 44
National Council of Churches 49
NECESSARY changes 11
Nestle and Aland 9, 48, 73
New American Standard Bible 43, 61, 68
new evangelicals 36
NEW GERMAN system 47
New Greek Text 11, 12, 15, 17, 19, 29, 32, 46, 75
New King James Version 9, 39, 52
New Revised English Bible 35
New Scofield Reference Bible 43, 61
Nida 38

nineteen thousand quotations from the gospels 54
NIV 16, 22, 27, 35, 37, 39, 43, 49, 55, 61, 62
NIV John 17:4 22
noblest literary work 18
noblest literary work in the Anglo-Saxon language 18
non-KJV-only view 45
Northern Baptist Convention 37, 56
notes of truth 7
November 3-4, 1978 5
Novum Testamentum Graece 9, 48, 73
OLD ENGLISH school 47
Olsen 38
Omaha Baptist Bible College 41
one, two, three, four or five 83
only acceptable English Bible 70
Origen 82
Orthodoxy 45, 65
P-52 53
Palmer 13
Partisanship 35
Paul Baloche 58
pdf 5, 8, 40, 46-48, 51, 75
pedantic officiousness of the Revisers 23
Pentecostalism 57
Philadelphia 5
Philips 43, 67
Piper 69
plain and clear errors 31
Pluperfect 23
president of the Dean Burgon Society 7
Professor Butrin 42, 45
Project Gutenberg EBook 8, 46, 47
Protestant denominations 51
R. V. 22, 23
RBP 43, 62
Readers Digest Bible 3
Received Text 3, 6, 9, 16
Received Traditional Text 83
Redman 58

Regular Baptist Press 42, 43, 61, 62
regurgitates 55
Resolutions adopted by the Convocation 30
Respectability of Witnesses 7
Revised English Version 9
Revised Standard Version 3, 27, 28, 32, 42, 44, 51
Revised Version .... iii, 2, 4, 9, 16, 25, 29, 31, 33, 36
Revisers of 1611 13
revision 2, 4, 5, 7-11, 15, 17-19, 23, 25, 29-37, 42, 46-48, 77
Revision Committee 31
Revision of 1881 .... 15, 33-35
Revision Revised 2, 4, 5, 8, 35-37, 46, 47, 77
Revisionists 10, 11, 14-16, 18, 20, 23-29, 34
rigid adherence 20
rival Translation 18
Roman Catholic 3, 51
Roman Catholic Cardinal 3
Romans 9:5 .... 26, 27
RSV 9, 42, 43, 49-51, 65, 73
Ruckman 1, 59
Rudolf Kittel 48, 49
Rule 11, 20, 24, 30
rule of translating 20, 24
RV John 17:4 22
Sacred Word 6
Saddleback 58
Samaritan Pentateuch 74
Sanborn .... ii, 36
Scholarly Myths 44
Scholarship 9, 25, 65
schoolboy method of translation 21
Science of Textual Criticism 6, 19
Scrivener 13, 29, 81
seldom 28
sending GARB church 39
separate 38
separation .... iii, 59
separatist 58
Septuagint 74

seven notes of truth	7
several Bibles	43, 61
Silva	68
Silvernale	38
Sinaiticus	53, 54
Smith	31, 33
Southern Baptist Convention	58, 59
St. Catherine	83
STANDING UPON THE ROCK	84
Stephen	81
Stephens	13
Stephens (1550)	13
Straub	5, 45
Strouse	44
Stunica	81
stupid harmonizer	16
superior	5, 68, 83
Syriac	53, 54, 74, 81
Syriac Bible	54
Syriac Church	81
Syriac Peshitta	74
taste	25
Tatian	54, 82
text of the nineteenth century	83
Textual Criticism	6, 19, 26, 44, 46, 47, 56
textual critics	45
textual preservation	70
Textus Receptus	3, 5, 7, 10, 15, 46, 62, 68, 81, 83
THE BIBLE	i-4, 15, 36-39, 48, 49, 51-53, 56, 59, 72, 74-76
The English Standard Version	iv, 9, 39, 40, 51, 61, 68
The Revised Version	9, 25, 29, 31, 36
The Revision Revised	2, 4, 5, 8, 35-37, 46, 47, 77
THE TRADITIONAL TEXT OF THE HOLY GOSPELS	6, 81, 83
three centuries	6
Tim Hughes	58
Tischendorf	14
Tomlin	58
tone, rhythm, and diction	17, 28
traditional hymns	40

Translation Philosophy .... iv, 71
Translation Review Scholars 65
TRINITY 32, 67-69
twelve countries 65
twenty denominations 65
Tyndale-King James legacy 73
UBS 3, 9, 38, 48, 73, 74
ultra-conservative 65
undermining of the King James Bible in GARB churches 56
Unger 48, 49
unintelligible 23
Unitarian 31-33
Unitarian Minister 31
Unitarian Smith 33
United Bible Societies 3, 9, 38, 73, 76
UNKNOWN DEPTHS OF SIN 42
untruth 3, 8
Valentinus 82
Vance Smith 31, 33
Variety of Evidence 7
Vaticanus 53, 54
Vernon Miller 62
VERSIONS .. 9, 11, 16, 17, 19, 27, 35, 36, 38, 39, 41, 43-47, 55, 56, 61-63, 71, 74, 76
very seldom 28
Viggo Olsen 38
Vulgate 53, 54, 74
W & H 9-11, 14-16, 19, 29, 32, 36, 69, 76
W&H 8, 12, 75, 81
Waite .... i-iii, 5, 7, 37, 48, 49, 75, 76
Wallace 5, 68, 69
Westcott 1, 4, 5, 8-10, 14, 15, 19, 35, 36, 42, 45-47, 75, 76
Westcott and Hort 4, 5, 14, 15, 19, 42, 46, 75, 76
Westcott and Hort's Greek text 4, 47
Western Baptist College in Oregon 59
Westminster Theological Seminary 68
Wheaton College 57, 66, 67
Wikgren 3
Wilberforce 32

William Tyndale 21
Williams 62
WORD Ministries 38
Word of GOD faithfully and helpfully 34
Word of God in English 3
Wordsworth 30
Wuest's Expanded Translation 43

Dean Burgon's Defense Of The AV
By Dr. David C. Bennett

King James Bible Defense Needed. We're living in a day and time when a proper understanding of the Authorized (King James) Version (AV) is missing both by its Gnostic Critical Greek Text and new version foes and its Ruckman and Riplinger following "friends."

Dean John Burgon To The Rescue. What greater defender of our Authorized Version to call upon but Dean John William Burgon, the Dean of Chichester in England. Dean Burgon was a Bible-believing scholar who was contemporary (and of the same denomination) with the two leading non-Bible-believing apostates, Bishop Westcott and Professor Hort. The views of these two leaders have been followed by many anti-KJB opponents of our day, including many theological conservatives.

Dr. Bennett Quotes Extensively From Dean Burgon. His quotations are from Dean Burgon's master work, *The Revision Revised* which has been reprinted by the Dean Burgon Society. It is available as BFT #595 @ $25.00 + $8.00 S&H. Dr. Bennett also exposes one of the current most erroneous followers of the Gnostic Critical Greek Text, the English Revised Version (ERV). An extensive INDEX aids the reader in finding key words and phrases.

Www.BibleForToday.org

BFT #4093   ISBN #978-1-56848-105-0

www.ingramcontent.com/pod-product-compliance
Lightning Source LLC
Chambersburg PA
CBHW062005040426
42447CB00010B/1915